Yl
You Can.

MAIN STREET

YES
You Can!

Joginder Singh
Former Director, CBI

MAIN STREET

Distributed by FULL CIRCLE & HPB

DISCLAIMER

This book is designed to provide practical ways to live a better life. It in no way serves as a substitute for professional counseling or therapy. Every effort has been made by the author, editor, and publisher to produce a complete and accurate book.

The purpose of this book is to motivate and inspire. The author and Main Street shall have neither liability nor responsibility to any person or entity with respect to any loss or damage caused, or alleged to have been caused, directly or indirectly, by the information contained in this book.

YES YOU CAN!
MAIN STREET
First Edition, August 2003
First Reprint, November 2003
ISBN 81-7621-144-3
© All Rights Reserved

Published by

| MAIN STREET |

and exclusively distributed in South Asia
by FULL CIRCLE & HPB
B-13, Sector 81, Noida, Phase II, U.P.
Tel: 95120-2563983
E-mail: gbp@del2.vsnl.net.in

Printed at Balaji Printers, Delhi-110032
PRINTED IN INDIA
03/03/02/11/21/SCANSET/SAP/BP/MBB

Its Good to Share

Ask any person what he wants in life. His answer will be to succeed in whatever venture he or she is engaged in. But ask the same person how many times he may have given up because a situation got too challenging and problematical and he did not want to spend the time or effort to do it in the way it needed to be done. In other words, such people have actually made the choice to not succeed, even though nobody wants to fail.

No excuse will do as success largely and perpetually is a matter of choices we make. You can chose to be a success, by choosing to deny yourself temporary pleasures and to put in the long hours that your aspiration and ambition requires. If some times, despite your best efforts you do not succeed, remember that the tree on the mountain accepts any weather nature brings. However, the only choice a tree has is putting down its roots, as deeply as possible. The same is true of human beings. Instead of surrendering yourself and your happiness, elect to honour your vision. If one advances confidently in the direction of ones' dreams, and endeavours to live the life which he or she has imagined, he will be successful. Always remember, that your own resolution to succeed is more important than anything else. The men who have done big things, are just women and men like you and me. The only difference is that they were not afraid to attempt big things, and were not afraid to risk failure in order to succeed.

Life lies in the living and is a sequence of instantaneous seconds and minutes. We can succeed only if we utilize each moment effectively and joyfully. Never discourage yourself, or allow others to discourage you about your dreams or your endeavours. All limits are self imposed. Eventually, what you determine not to do portrays your life, as much as, what you do select to do. The choice of being happy or otherwise is always available to us. Emerson said: "Big jobs usually go to men who prove their ability to outgrow small ones."

This book is a small contribution to the development of an individual. I have tremendously benefited by penning down my experiences, as, I hope, you would benefit by going through it. This is one book which you can read anywhere and mostly find your own experience reflected here. In fact, when I gave a chapter of this book to a friend for his comments, he asked me how I had put down in the book, what he was feeling all the time! Each chapter has a personal touch, as at one time or the other, I have gone through the experience described or tried the experiments on self improvement. As there can be no one solution for any trouble or problem, this book does not claim to solve all life's problems. It only suggests methods, which you can try and benefit from, only to the extent you want. Happy Reading and Cheers.

Joginder Singh
IPS (Retd.)
Former Director, CBI, India

CONTENTS

CONTENTS

1

TIME FOR
INTROSPECTION

One of the main reasons for failure in achieving goals is that we are looking in the wrong places for the solution to our problems and challenges. Generally speaking, the answer does not lie where a large majority of people search for it. We may have a particular problem but the problem itself should not be the reason for choosing a wrong solution. Life in a rut suits most people as they do not want to face or come to grips with the truth about their problems, their lives and themselves. We have to face the fact that no matter what has happened to us in the past or what we are facing now is of our own making. It is up to each one of us to take responsibility for our own lives and happiness. It is for us to do something constructive and positive for ourselves. People dwell too much on the negative in their lives. They also conduct extensive post-mortems as to what went wrong instead of trying to see the positive side of things in the present. It is for us to touch those positive events and make them flower. It is our thoughts which determine our feelings and these in turn direct our actions. For example, if you are always feeling depressed and thinking, "I'll never be successful and happy" this thought will produce feelings of despair and hopelessness. Consequently, you unconsciously go on doing something or the other which will reinforce this belief and thought. Thus, you do not try to do anything which will improve your relationship with others or your performance at work. This vicious circle prevents you from doing anything constructive. It also confirms your belief that it is not worth trying to change or improve things as nothing is going to happen. This cycle continues and you are neither happy nor do the problems that you are facing get solved. Thus, destructive thoughts keep on having a hold on you. Unhappiness and difficulties become a part and parcel of life and the individual feels that there is no escape for him or her.

★ **Accept challenges which come your way.** The solution is to identify your depressing and destructive thoughts. Take action to transform them into positive energy before they dominate and depress you. Consciously replace negative attitude with a more realistic and positive outlook. In this manner you can take control of your thoughts and emotions which will enable you to live your life to the fullest.

Spot the thoughts that are preventing you from realizing your dreams. By ridding yourself of unhappy thoughts you will be able to manage your life in a much better way. Do not believe anybody if they tell you that ignoring a problem or a situation is the easy way out. In the long run you will end up being trapped in situations which are both painful and stressful. Always be on the look out for crossing new frontiers. This is the only way in which you will know your strengths and capabilities. Accept challenges which come your way.

Do Not Ignore Difficulties — Face Them

Sometimes a difficult situation worsens with time. It calls for resolution one way or the other. Sometimes a long wait can mellow a problem but it is rarely the case that nothing needs to be done. Waiting is one way of escaping as it means not confronting your fears and not making a change. It is a universal desire to stick to comfort zones as it means avoiding all challenges and difficulties and continuing with the status quo. Each challenge in our life is capable of giving us strength, wisdom and opportunity for further progress. We can learn from life each moment and work for our rewards. Do not wait too long in the hope that you will not have to make a change. Life is in a state of flux. Whether you like it or not, you will confront challenge after challenge in life. Only by learning to meet challenges do you get a chance to learn and grow.

Do not talk yourself into avoiding situations and putting up with any depressing or humiliating ones. This is dangerous thinking especially when it is related to something that is making you very unhappy. Face situations, however harmful they may be, and find solutions, however difficult. Never take anything lying down in your life. Events and situations which make you unhappy and doubt your own competence and strength should be put aside. Do not give up on yourself and your dreams because you feel helpless and unable to control your life. Live the way you want to, the way you really should. Believe in yourself. Choose your strategies for dealing with your problems. Put in the required efforts in your fight for a cause or in your struggle for an achievement. Never compromise on your pride, your self-esteem, struggle for a cause or a promotion that you feel is your due. Never hesitate to stand up for yourself and for your happiness. There is always something that you can do about your happiness. Putting up with a bad situation even for a little while can turn into a lifetime of shattered dreams and hopes.

★ You have to take care of your own unhappiness and stress in your life. Nobody else is going to solve your problems.

What is causing you unhappiness? Most of us tend to blame something or somebody for our unhappiness whether it is our health, weight, shyness, lack of money or dissatisfaction with the current assignment. This keeps us from locating and realizing the real reason for our unhappiness. Excuses or self-justifications are merely symptoms and not the true causes of unhappiness. Let us, for example, examine the real reasons for ill health or obesity. Is it because you do not eat healthy food or eat a lot of junk food? Or is it because you do not spend any time keeping yourself fit by exercising? A close examination and self-introspection will indicate the true reasons. Then it will be up to you to plan remedial action directed at taking care of yourself. It is one thing to identify the reason and symptom for a lapse. It is entirely a different matter to take remedial action. One often stated reason for this kind of situation is that a heavy work schedule does not give you time for eating a balanced diet and exercising regularly. The solution for this kind of situation is to manage your time well. Plan your lifestyle and work in such a way that you can eat more healthy food and exercise regularly. You have to take care of your own unhappiness and stress in your life. Nobody else is going to solve your problems.

Learn from your past. Do not ignore the way you are and analyze why you continue repeating the same mistakes. Do not be trapped in patterns of unhappiness, and unstable behaviour. Do not be enslaved by past behaviour patterns. Accept and understand past mistakes so that you can learn from them in the present. This will help you avoid past emotional mistakes, pain, professional blunders and other causes of unhappiness. This is the only way by which you can uncover the reasons for past mistakes and learn lessons for the future as well. Never hesitate in examining the reasons as to why you keep on making the same mistakes again and again. Is it because of negative people and bad experiences which have plagued you for a long time? Is it because you have been taught to feel negative about yourself and see the world through pessimistic glasses? If you do your best, whatever happens will be for the best. Our core beliefs about our happiness and ourselves have been formed under the influence of our parents, teachers, siblings, peers and friends during the various stages of our life, from infancy to adulthood.

We have learnt many habits and developed all sorts of expectations. We have become a composite personality under their influence and on account of our experiences. It is for this reason that we must review our past. We cannot change it or run away. Challenge yourself if you are thinking and feeling depressed. This is the only way you can change your approach to life, your convictions, your beliefs and your behaviour.

2

THE ART OF
SUCCESS

How is it that some people achieve whatever goals they set for themselves while others stumble and crumble at every step? How is it that there are some winners and others are losers? To become a winner it is very important to find the right answers to this question. There are certain qualities or techniques which anybody can use to achieve success and reach desired goals. The lives and qualities of successful people are the best beacon lights to success. It is not necessary that only a degree and formal college education will equip you to succeed in life. Abraham Lincoln was self-educated. He acquired his education by borrowing books and reading them under the streetlights or by the light of a fire. Benjamin Franklin did not attend any school. The Wright brothers were no scientists. They were bicycle mechanics by profession. Yet they succeeded in giving the world the aeroplane. Success also does not necessarily depend upon one's heredity and environment.

It is the result of inspiration, aspiration, desperation and perspiration. Your luck generally changes as a result of the above inputs. There is always a fierce struggle on the road leading to your desired goal. No triumph comes without effort and changing obstacles into tools for success. No smooth sea has ever made a successful and a skilful mariner. For achieving your desired goal you must have a fierce and a strong desire to succeed. Success begins in the mind. Whatever the mind of man can believe and conceive it can achieve. You should make a commitment to yourself to succeed. Do not believe that success is the result of either an accident or a fluke. Nothing is ever achieved without working for it with integrity, wisdom, commitment and a success-oriented attitude. You have to accept responsibility for your decisions which will ultimately determine your destiny. Make your work and reaching your goals a delight. The best way to succeed is to accept and learn from your mistakes. It is a fact that luck only follows hard work. Master the fundamentals of whatever you are required to do. Keep on developing your character, confidence, values, beliefs and personality by always keeping in view the examples and lives of successful people. You will notice that all successful people combine in themselves integrity, unselfishness, patience, understanding, conviction, courage, loyalty and self-esteem. They have both ability and character. Hence, they are successful in whatever they undertake.

No success is possible unless you believe that you can succeed. Positive faith in yourself is both vital and crucial for success. This attitude will help your competence reach visibly successful levels of performance and prepare you for hard work. An optimistic approach is the sine qua non of success.

★
No success is
possible unless
you believe that
you can succeed.

Never look at the clock when you set out to achieve your goal. Look at the task and ask yourself whether your output can be further improved. There is little room at the top. The top is always rarefied and limited space. Only one person can be there at a time. Do not be the one who gets left out for want of persistence, determination and commitment. Mediocres and shirkers fall by the way. Never be a quitter because a quitter can never be a winner. The difference between success and failure is only a few minutes or a few hours everyday. You have to keep on striving for success and happiness at every conceivable opportunity. The difference between success and failure is your attitude towards success and the strategies that you employ to achieve it. Never postpone your happiness and zest for life and work. You should make it a habit to enjoy your profession and your job all the time.

Leo Tolstoy wrote, "People live not by the reason of any care they have for themselves but by the love for them that is in other people." Have only those people for friends, companions and lovers who do their best to bring out the best in you. They will be of unlimited worth to you. Such persons understand what life means to you and your goals. They feel for you as you feel for yourselves. They are the ones who are bound to you in triumph and disaster. They provide a purpose to live and break the spell of loneliness. A true friend is worth befriending as he will always stand by you. But before you expect others to be the right person to be your friend you must also become one. Help each other towards achieving your respective goals. To love and to be loved is the greatest happiness of existence. If you are happy, the hard journey on the road to success becomes pleasurable. Live your life kingsize. Just live it and never lose sight of your goal.

During a congregational service once a priest asked that all those desiring to go to heaven should stand up. All arose except Abraham Lincoln who was also in the congregation. Then the priest said that all those who did not want to go to hell should arise. Lincoln still remained seated. The priest was perplexed and asked him as to where he wanted to go. Lincoln calmly said, "I want to go to Congress."

Be always committed to your cause. Be so engrossed in your work that you have hardly any time to think of anything else. The great secret of success is to do whatever you are to do and do it wholeheartedly. For many persons happiness remains a chimera. However, it comes to those who seek it in their work and do not specifically look for it. Happiness is not something which can be felt or experienced at a given moment. It is in a sense the quality of a whole life. It is a happy life which is a fulfilled and a purposeful life. Happiness is a state of mind. It is not an absolute or a tangible concept. It is not something which can be considered in isolation. It varies from person to person. It has a lot to do with faith, hope, courage and ideals to live by. By and large fear, uncertainty, confusion and greed are the causes of much unhappiness and failure. But we have it in our power to meet the greatest challenge of our time. Plato defines happiness in terms of harmony within the soul. He

> "Happiness is a state of which one is unconscious. It is only later when misery strikes does one realize how happy one was."
>
> J. Krishnamurti

equates it with the spiritual well-being of a truly virtuous man. Immanuel Kant, a pessimist, did not approve of the idea of happiness. He regarded the pursuit of one's own happiness a self-centred act motivated by narrow considerations. According to J. Krishnamurti: "Happiness is a state of which one is unconscious. It is only later when misery strikes does one realize how happy one was."

One need not entirely accept what earlier thinkers have said or felt about happiness. It is ultimately our own perceptions and attitude to life which matter. Two persons in similar circumstances may not exactly be happy or unhappy. They may not be on the same wavelength and their expectations may be different. Swami Vivekanand said that the goal of man should not be to seek happiness or to avoid misery but to go to the root of it all and master the situation which is responsible for their creation. It is absolutely necessary to overcome the negative and harmful thought waves by countering them with good benign waves and adopt a positive approach. If the water of a lagoon is dirty, the bottom is not visible. Similarly, only when the mind is positive, clear and tranquil can it lead us to victory.

Secrets Of Success

Make yourself the star of your workplace. For this you must have clear and precise objectives to be achieved within a definite time-frame. Always respect and value time. Be result-oriented and keep track of the hours. Monitor every minute of your professional and leisure time. Respect the time of others as well as your own. Be always organized and write down everything you want to accomplish. Keep a list of your objectives, your lists of tasks to be done and your daily planners with you. Prioritize and approach your tasks in a descending order of importance. The most important work should get the highest priority in the day's agenda. Other items should follow. Always focus on the task at hand. Each task should be given undivided attention. Do not clutter your mind with the things that could be done later or things already completed in the past. Simply concentrate on the task at hand. But before taking up a task make sure that it fits in well within your overall long-term objectives. It should be worth your time and attention. Chalk out a strategy for attaining your objectives successfully. Always be on the look out for methods to improve your working. Update your skills constantly. You cannot do everything. Delegation of some tasks is one method of accomplishing more.

You cannot always be successful. Hone your judgement and know when to quit. If you can do this, you will know when to call it quits and move forward without any anxiety, tension or guilt. Flexibility is a great quality. Result-oriented people are realists. Time is not something solid. It is fluid. Like everything in life, schedules change constantly. Achievers get pleasure from shuffling tasks and still meeting their obligations on time. You can develop the habit of getting results from your efforts. It is a question of developing skills through practice. Check yesterday's list against today's reality to assess how close you are to the goals you have set for yourself.

Always make an assessment of yesterday's 'To Do' list to crosscheck how realistic it has turned out to be today. This will help you to avoid or rectify mistakes, if any, in your planning. Keep on visualizing your goals and lists of the tasks to be done. Close your eyes and view yourself doing the activity that you have chosen. Determine how long will it take and assess your odds of success. Do this for every activity on your 'To Do' list. This will enable you to modify, if necessary, your schedule in the light of changing priorities and make it more realistic Get into the habit of setting daily goals, achieving them and experiencing the thrill of fulfilment. Shut the door on frequent interruptions and disturbances. Always try to be more productive and have a system to find out whether your efforts are generating an output in proportion to the amount of time you are spending on a particular task or a project. It is best to time your tasks either with a stop-watch or by logging time for each task throughout the day. I prefer to use two watches and one of them is always in the stop watch mode so that I am fully conscious of the time I should spend on exercise, a dinner or any other social function. Pay attention to the clock and regulate your timings. Work on your doubts which is another name for 'buts'. We all have them. For improving your results and skills, identify and address your personal 'buts'. The more you can eliminate such angularities, the better and smoother your life will become. Always aim at making a contribution. 'Self-police' the meetings you attend by asking yourself, "How can I contribute more? Am I contributing anything worthwhile to such meetings?" Be fully prepared so that you can make a substantive contribution whether it is at meetings or social functions.

Remind yourself of your goals. Read them aloud every day to make them tangible and personal. This way you will be able to maintain a high level of motivation.

Aim To Do Your Best

Most of the time we pressurize ourselves and our life to achieve perfection. We strive to have perfect children, perfect houses, perfect husbands or perfect wives and a perfect work environment, unfortunately, in an imperfect world. It is just not possible to be perfect all the time. This approach can sabotage our life as well as delay achieving our ambitions or fulfilling dreams as we wait for perfect conditions. Absolute perfection exists only in our imagination. On the one hand it can keep us from working to realize our dreams because we are waiting for everything to be 'just right'. On the other hand, even if we do achieve our dreams we might think that our efforts were not good enough. In our minds we will still feel as if we have failed because we think that we could have done better.

It is good to aim at perfection but it should not be pursued to such an extent that it destroys your chances of happiness. It should not prevent you from working towards your, ambitions and dreams. It should be followed in a way that does not strip away your confidence and feeling of achievement of anything you might have attained. Do not allow the quest for perfection to ruin your life because whatever you do you will always feel that you could have done better. Never be harsh on yourself. Make your standards and goals realistic. Always keep yourself alert. Set the bottomlines as to what you can live with and what you can do without. Ask yourself the question whether you are trying to prove anything to yourself or to others? Only self-introspection can make you perfect and rid you of your apprehensions. Do not allow happiness-destroying thoughts to stand between you and your success.

Ascertain the reasons why you have not realized your dreams so far. Study your behaviour and the steps you should take to tackle difficult circumstances and your difficult feelings. Once you take concrete steps to face your depressing feelings you can change your life as well as your restricting approach to any stressful behaviour. Always be on the look out to learn about yourself by examining your past performance and actions. This process will enable you to change your beliefs and behaviour. Remember that life is beautiful. Have faith in it and in your yourself. Keep your faith all the time. Remember that the sun may remain hidden only for a little while and spring will certainly come.

★
> Do not allow the quest for perfection to ruin your life because whatever you do you will always feel that you could have done better.

Opportunities Are Knocking All The Time — Get Up And Open The Door

Opportunities are never served on a platter. They are there all the time. You have to spot them and use them for your success. Initiative is essential to get you there first. Be ready to take calculated risks if necessary. Many unspotted opportunities are like those flowers that are born to blush and wither unseen. Opportunities afford a chance to display your leadership skills. Developing the qualities necessary for success is not difficult if you will it. You have to commit yourself to your goal. You need to convince yourself that you can do it. You have to be committed to take up the challenge of rising to the top.

Be The Best Edition Of Yourself

Shakespeare said that nothing is good or bad but thinking makes it so. All joys, pleasures and miseries have their origin in the mind. It is for each one of us to decide whether we wire ourselves for happiness or misery. Happiness certainly does not dwell in a bottle of whisky or in a wad of currency notes. Happiness is an approach to life founded upon certain basic values and plan of living. It is a condition of the mind. It has its roots in human conduct. Generally speaking, a clean life and adherence to ideals of excellence in human conduct produce happiness. This condition in turn is responsible for good health and general well-being. It is the source of cheerfulness and glow in you. Riches cannot 'buy' happiness. The heart and mind cannot feed on luxury goods. Affection does not thrive on luxuries. Human nature is such that if you make up your mind you can be happy anywhere. Half-naked, underfed and undernourished labourers, working on construction projects, men and women carrying loads are happy singing joyous songs.

The real joy of life lies in your work and performance. Never rob yourselves of happiness by postponing it. Happiness is not a destination to arrive at. It is a journey. Any opportunity is a good reason to enjoy the blessings of life. The secret is to live in and for the present. You do not need astrologers, palmists soothsayers and pseudo-saints to tell you all this. Such people simply 'rob' you of your will-power and direction by suggesting charms, recitations or some other method of warding off bad luck. They are interested in your wads of crisp currency notes so that they can sell 'hope' to you.

You have to condition yourself to purposeful living by substituting good habits for bad habits. Create positive patterns of behaviour. Find out what is holding you back and what is pushing you into distress and disappointment. Then discard the negative thoughts and situations. This can be done only by changing your thinking and concentrating on the noble and positive aspects of life. This is the only way in which you can transform yourself into a new person. Be objective in examining your behaviour patterns which have been for a long time in your life. Unhappiness is as much a habit as happiness is. Worry needs to be blown out of your life. It can and should be done. You have only to will it. Irritations and tensions blur happiness. They are the results of long held repugnant thought patterns. Understand why you are doing what you are doing. Analyze what is coming in the way of your success. This is the first step in transforming yourself.

There are a number of reasons for 'fits' of unhappiness. These include blues, helplessness, timidity and hostile people who would like to pull you down. If you are successful in pinning down the causes, then half the battle in shedding gloom and despair is already won. You have the power to encash your abilities. You should do it by all means at your command. Plenty of money, a palatial house, a fleet of cars and a beautiful

> ★ Unhappiness is as much a habit as happiness is.

wife do not guarantee happiness. There is no amulet which can materialize happiness. Happiness is closely allied with and depends upon our actions. A life of inactivity leads to a life of decay and putrefaction. Action is the only glorious principle of life. It is the only one that saves us from stagnation and unhappiness. Dedicating yourself to a noble cause reveals the highest levels of character in human beings. The grand edifice of civilization is an eloquent testimony to what noble endeavours can achieve. Monuments of civilization have been erected and built by character and hard work. Never be idle. Idleness is the refuge of the weak and the feeble. It leads to misery. Idleness cannot give that feeling of well-being which springs from active participation in life's activities. Action in life is as essential as time-keeping is to a watch.

Action is invigorating. It is a tonic. There is no happiness greater than that which stems from the use of your physical, mental and intellectual faculties. Health and happiness have numerous foes. Worry is in the frontline to destroy happiness. It stimulates morbid and miserable feelings. The solution to this problem does not lie in pushing worry under the carpet. You should enjoy life and not suffer it.

The following suggestions will help in overcoming stress and worries. Review your past to pinpoint the 'misery' areas. Do your best to get rid of them. It is not difficult to throw them out of your life. However, the most difficult part is their identification.

Tension and worries are threat signals. Learn to spot them so that when they come you can tell yourself that they are a temporary and a momentary phenomenon. The moment they disappear, unhappiness also disappears. Never give way to moodiness and depression. Depression is the expression of self-dislike or self-disrespect. In this condition it is not others who are bothering you. It is only your own self wallowing in misery. Address your inner self and you will get amazing results.

There is greater happiness in giving than in receiving. We have to face a certain amount of stress in our lives. The trick lies in taking it easy. Life in the fast lane has its own hazards. A major one is stress. Stress and unhappiness always emerge out of what we have done or are doing. They can lead to listlessness and disinterest in life. There can be strange reactions because of stress including overeating and screaming at others. A stressful situation is like a pressure cooker which is about to burst. A job switch may help but not always even though the new job may be less demanding.

Stress can be and is generally job related. It can also be travel related. But an interesting and exciting work and approach to life can mitigate it. Each one of us has his or her own level of tolerance vis-à-vis stress. Working in high-pressured jobs, trying to live up to the expectations of your superiors, increasing competition and always living under the threat of being sacked for not performing well is bound to add to the stress. Feeling dissatisfied with one's work, getting unnecessarily nervous, anxious, angry, unhappy and annoyed at even the most trivial matters are indications of stress. Stress manifests itself from your own self and radiates to those around you.

★ **Each one of us has the capacity and capability to convert stress into a positive factor to achieve more than what we have done so far.**

Maintaining performance and achievement levels can also be the cause of stress. Stress can graduate from nail biting, grinding teeth and tapping feet to serious illnesses like a heart attack, ulcers, diabetes, depression, asthma, alcoholism etc. When the mind is not able to control itself the stress follows. It has nothing to do with external situations. It is important not to look for stress in the wrong places. In today's fast paced and dog-eat-dog world, stress levels can assume alarming proportions. A stress-free approach and environment boosts morale, increases productivity and facilitates positive lifestyle changes. Stress is a non-specific response of the body to any abnormal demand made upon it. It puts life out of balance. It leads to disequilibrium. It is a physiological phenomenon. It is also a reflection of challenges exceeding a person's ability to cope. It is left to each one of us to determine not to allow circumstances and stress to get the better of us or overwhelm us. Each one of us has the capacity and capability to convert stress into a positive factor to achieve more than what we have done so far. However, each one of us needs to devise his own stress management program to convert the minus into a plus.

Celebrate Life

Quite often some people belittle the world and its charms saying that all is lost and there is no sweetness in life. This attitude is surprising when there are still sunshine, rain, roses, spring, autumn, stars, honey, good friends and caring families. Good humour and good nature is there in abundance in and about all of us. You can extract the best out of everything. It is only a question of being dedicated about doing what you want to do. It is also a question of understanding your own behaviour towards others and managing yourself and your relationships with others. You cannot do everything you want to in life. However, you can do some things. That what you can do you ought to do. Each day is too short for all we want to accomplish whether it is reading, writing or meeting all the friends we want to. In fact, I find that I can finish only about fifty percent of the things I plan to do because of lack of time. You should keep a record of your measurements, achievements and setbacks so that you know what you should do and what you should avoid. Life is a series of surprises. It is this element which makes it interesting and keeps it going. The following anonymous poem sums up the situation:

> This day is mine to mar or make
> God keep me strong and true
> Let me no erring by-path take
> No erring actions do.
> Grant me when the setting sun
> This fleeting day shall end
> I may rejoice over something done
> Be richer by a friend.
> Let all I meet along the way
> Speak well of me tonight.
> I would not have the humblest say;
> I had hurt him by a slight.
> Let there be something true and fine
> When night slips down to tell
> That I have lived this day of mine
> Not selfishly but well.

It is the maximum good and minimum friction that is important. Nobody reaches the top without occasionally slipping. When someone stumbles give him a chance and get him moving again. As a person determined to succeed you should establish clear achievable objectives for your performance as well as those of your organization. You should find ways and means to reach and touch everybody in your team and organization. In any job you will find a number of so-called experts. Do not be overawed or bewildered by them or their expertise. More often than not your own judgement is better than that of the experts. Quite often people will complain against you. This is due to the fact that you want to give your best and expect others to give their best, too. If you are a hard worker and a hard taskmaster you will drive people towards high standards of performance and will expect a great deal from them. This approach will not make you popular especially with those who do not work or do not like to work hard but it should not deter you from setting high standards and goals and achieving them.

Ultimately, everybody likes to win. Everybody loves a winner. This can be seen in all the pages of the newspapers. You will be respected as a successful leader if you help others to reach great heights and achieve worthwhile objectives. As an individual committed to achieve success you have to devise your own set of rules and guidelines for successful living. During the course of the day you will come across a number of ideas for efficient working. The problem arises later on when you want to recollect and act upon them. You can determine your own method for storing and recalling them whether it is in a notebook or in a computer or a memo pad. What is important is to have a sound system of recalling and acting on ideas.

Do not be afraid of mistakes and misjudgements. They teach you a great deal and lead you to victory. My own method is to speak the idea or the work to be done in a portable mini cassette recorder or jot it down. Even if an idea occurs to me at midnight it is immediately put on tape. (Otherwise for the whole night I go on thinking of how to do it but when the morning comes it disappears from the mind.) If I do not put it on record, then it goes on haunting me. (This way I can get it out of my mind and store it for action next day.) If it is not put in some kind of a memory bank immediately the chances are that it will elude you when you want to act on it.

You should be an active participant in the dramas of real life. Face whatever comes your way. Remember that sometimes you may be criticized even for doing just and correct things. Your best defence should be the armour of indifference. It is a very effective shield against even the most biting and sarcastic criticism. In the face of such criticism never lose your zest or enthusiasm for life. The creative power of enthusiasm can do wonders for you. Being enthusiastic can lead you to good health. Depressive thoughts affect optimism, faith and a positive, productive lifestyle. The only way to be enthusiastic, is just to think enthusiastic, feel enthusiastic and act enthusiastic. It is the same for courage. You can be courageous just by being courageous and overcoming your fears. Forcing yourself to be happy will make you happy. You can get ahead in life only by being enthusiastic. Never minimize your work or opportunities that come your way. Never berate yourself and your work. Enthusiasm is a good indicator about the quality of life you lead or can lead or will lead. Avoid giving way to annoyance or irritation.

★ • • • • • • • • • • • • •
• **Destiny is calling**
• **each one of us**
• **every day.**
• • • • • • • • • • • • • •

Take things as they come. Be urbane and philosophical. Accept the problems that come in your life. Discover the best possible solution to deal with them. If one door closes, another one opens. Do not waste time in regret over closed doors or methods. Regret or guilt does not yield any results. Instead, open another door or find another method for solving your problems. You should clearly view the resources and the opportunities that are available to you. Treat the problems as opportunities. See the best in every situation. Expect the best at all times. Destiny is calling each one of us every day. Every day can be a great day if you do not waste time in futile recrimination. Never even think of, "If only I had done this or that." This will remind you only of past failures, errors of judgements and mistakes which are best forgotten. Failures and failure-producing thoughts should be cut out of your life. Expect the best at all times even in the worst of situations. Cast out of your life all negative and depressing thoughts. Embrace the positive and throw away defeatist concepts. Remind yourself that you are better than what you think you can be. Clem Stone says, "Millions of people in every walk of life have never tried to achieve high goals that were achievable. Why? They were told or believed, 'It can't be done.'" And they never learned or applied the first principle of the art of motivation, that is to say, a positive mental attitude (PMA) could have helped them achieve any goal that did not violate universal laws, the laws of God and the rights or goals of their fellowmen. If only they had motivated themselves to Recognise, Relate, Assimilate and Apply from what they read, heard, saw, thought and experienced... The subconscious will come up with the answers through repetition and repetition.

> "Millions of people in every walk of life have never tried to achieve high goals that were achievable. Why? They were told or believed, 'It can't be done.'"

You have to believe in your own judgement. You have to trust yourself to make decisions without bothering whether others approve of your approach. Never try to be somebody you are not. It is very stressful to be a different person from what you actually are. It is a wonder of wonders that most people think that events and things that happen to them happen only to them and not to the rest of the world. Never lie to yourself. It is more pernicious than the lies and untruths you can tell others. Appearances are crucial to success and dressing well is very important. Occasionally, you have to be ready to be cheated by deceptive appearances. For achieving success there are some basic premises which should be kept in mind all the time. One: What are the ground rules of the game or plan? Learn them and master them. Two: Who is responsible for enforcing the same? What can be your role in that? Three: Who is the boss? Are you trying to be one or help him? Is it he or somebody else who is responsible for enforcing the same?

You must decide your bottomline or *'lakshman rekha'* as the scriptures put it and never cross it. You have to defend your honour. If you do not, you will give an impression that you have none to defend. It is a paradox that it is not the work which exhausts the mind but idleness. Thoughts are fragrant like flowers that sweeten our lives. Whatever we sow in life, we reap the same. It is the higher view which will drive away the baser instincts from life. If you do the right action you will be able to do the greatest good with the minimum of energy and strain. The effort should be to

> Say to yourself, "Nothing is impossible for me. I have the strength and intelligence of the gods."

keep the lower instincts under check. They cause chaos in life. With sound character and God's rhythm in life, order and harmony will come naturally to you. As a high achiever you should have a sense of being a higher self. You can accomplish many amazing feats by believing in your capacity to achieve anything you wish to achieve. You should not set any limits to your knowledge. Never place a limitation on it. Just plunge headlong into well-thought out activity which will lead to the achievement of your goals. Believe in yourself to the point of being able to control the conditions and circumstances around you. Say to yourself, "Nothing is impossible for me. I have the strength and intelligence of the gods." Reducing stress and resistance will increase your efficiency. When you are in harmony with yourself and the universe, all factors in your life will function as one entity. When you are in rhythm, you can have the highest level of efficiency. For a top class performance you really have to be a happy individual. Says Thomas Carlyle: "Give me a man who sings at his work." It is the deep and vibrant joy which can make you efficient. You can train yourself to live joyfully only by thinking and practising joy. Think regularly and persistently on the things you desire. In this way you can make yourself any type of a person whether a great achiever or a courageous or a joyful person.

Put joyful and glorious thoughts in your mind. You can improve yourself only by controlling and channelizing your mind in the direction you desire. Dwell only on happy, healthy and helpful thoughts. Condition your mind with optimistic thinking and affirmations. The Law of Reciprocity works in life in all directions and all the time. In exact proportion to the amount of joy and happiness you spread and the help you give others you will receive those back. Being joyful and dynamic are essential qualities to success. Condition your thoughts to live on the top. With success thoughts saturating you, you will always be on the top. Replace your destructive and depressing thoughts with positive and uplifting thoughts. Dwell only on your victories and successes. Close the door on your past failures, regrets or bitter, unpleasant experiences. Cut out all negative and ugly influences. You should develop a strong motivating force as well as an intense desire and a belief to reach your desired goal. It is true that, occasionally, a lot of life's problems will gang up against us but you should never give up your positive attitude. Otherwise that itself will become a handicap in overcoming your difficulties. Always imagine yourself as a successful person. You can be what you think yourself to be.

Be Hopeful

God has made all human beings alike. At the same time He has endowed each one of us with different qualities. It is up to each one of us to develop higher qualities or to yield to baser instincts. The choice is entirely ours. Be always optimistic and hopeful. Hope even impossible hopes. Dream big dreams. It is this attitude in life, which will fill you with courage and resourcefulness. Never worry or complain of injustice either to yourself or to others. Instead try to strengthen yourself with right values. A sense of proportion is essential for helping yourself and others whenever any help is required. You should live your life on the pattern of a lighthouse. It shows the path to ships and boats as they pass by. Your life should glow so that others can walk on their paths in its light. For success it is essential to have an accurate self-assessment. It is only by assessing yourself correctly that you can increase your competence. You should identify themes and patterns of your organization clearly. Always be clear and inspiring to your team.

It is only by your example that you can effectively inspire your team to work with pride and dedication. As a leader be creative. Praise people for trying even if they do not succeed. Shower praise at every opportunity. Praise is nutrition for the ego. It is a powerful tool. Not only do people want success and material goods they also want these to be noticed. It is only for this reason that people buy clothes and big houses. Everybody wants to be complimented for what he does. Recognition for accomplishments is a great incentive. President Theodore Roosevelt said, "It is not the critic who counts; not the man who points out how the strong man stumbled or where the doer of the deeds could have done better. The credit belongs to the man who is actually in the arena; whose face is marred by dust, sweat and blood; who strives valiantly; who errs and comes short again and again; who knows the great enthusiasms, the great devotions and spends himself in a worthy cause; who at the best knows in the end the triumph of high achievement; and who, at the worst, if he fails at least fails while daring greatly; so that his place shall be never with those cold and timid souls who know neither victory nor defeat." There is an inspiring poem on the subject:

> The test of a man is the fight he makes
> The grit he daily shows;
> In the face of

Fate's numerous bumps and blows
A coward can smile when to stand up and cheer
While some other fellow stares.
It is not the victory after all
But the fight that brother makes;
The man who driven against the wall
Still stands up erect and takes
The blows of fate with his head held high;
Bleeding, bruised and pale
Is the man who'll win in the by and by
For he isn't afraid to fail.
It is the bumps you get and the jolts you get
And the shocks that your courage stands
The hours of sorrow and vain regret
The prize that escapes your hands
That test your mettle and proves your worth
It isn't the blows you deal
But the blows you take on the good old earth.
That shows if your stuff is real.

It is a paradox that your society, friends and relatives want you to achieve great heights. But at the same time they want you to conform to existing values. Conformity is nothing but steamrolling your approach to life as well as to your creative thinking. It closes all doors to new avenues. Thinking and acting creative are synonymous though many may not agree with that definition. A well-conceived thought leads to constructive achievements. You have to tread the path to creativity through hard work and enthusiasm. You have to be prepared to tread on the corns of others if necessary. This approach can lead to problems and dangers. You should not be apologetic if you do something out of the ordinary to fulfil your ideas. Human beings are the greatest assets in the success of any undertaking. It is this asset which turns barren lands, raw materials like wood, cement and steel into buildings, factories, commerce and industry. Every person has a unique character, special skills and attitudes. Combinations of several factors and the proficiency of the individuals only can lead to achievement. Managing human assets is both an art and a science. A manager has to have a total commitment to his work before he can demand it from his employees. The successful leader ensures a high morale in his team. He motivates his colleagues and subordinates to give their best. He should learn to face confrontations, slammed doors and storm warnings with equanimity. A leader leads by accepting mistakes. He does not blame his boss or subordinates. He is strong in mental gymnastics. Imagining as to what will be the outcome of a particular course of action can prevent conflict. A leader has to set long-term, medium and short-term objectives for the organization for which he is working. The setting of the objectives also involves the management style as well as the culture and the tone of the organization. He should be able to visualize and communicate the objectives of the organization. A leader needs to keep himself physically fit. Leadership demands emotional, physical and intellectual activity. About the complaint that there is too much struggle in life which takes away happiness, a poet says:

Tell me not in mournful numbers
Life is but an empty dream!
For the soul is dead that slumbers
And things are not what they seem.

Life is real! Life is earnest!
And the grave is not its goal:
Dust thou art to dust returnest
Was not spoken of the soul.
Not enjoyment and not sorrow
Is our destined end or way:
But to act that each tomorrow
Find us farther than today.
Art is long and Time is fleeting
And our hearts though stout and brave
Still like muffled drums are beating
Funeral marches to the grave.
In the world's broad field of battle
In the bivouac of life
Be not like dumb driven cattle!
Be a hero in the strife!
Trust no Future however pleasant!
Let the dead past bury its dead!
Act-act in the living present!
Lives of great men all remind us
We can make our lives sublime
And departing leave behind us
Footprints on the sands of time:
Footprints that perhaps another
Sailing over life's solemn main
A forlorn and shipwrecked brother
Seeing shall take heart again.
Let us then be up and doing
With a heart for any fate;
Still achieving, still pursuing
Learn to labour and to wait.

And let the face of God shine through.
But East and West will pinch the heart
That cannot keep them pushed apart;
And he whose soul is flat — the sky
Will cave in on him by and by.

Most people can be and are about as happy as they wish to be. Very little is needed to make a happy life. It is all within ourselves and in our way of thinking. The spoken word, the released arrow, the past life and the neglected opportunity cannot be retrieved and it does not serve any purpose to lament over them. The best course is to make the best of the present and be determined to enjoy it.

3

ORGANIZING FOR SUCCESS

Goals and Vision

Every event, every incident and, in fact, everyone has a purpose in life. Each one of us has a unique or special talent. When we blend this unique talent with service to others we experience an ecstasy and exultation in our lives. This may be expressed or unexpressed and is the goal which we cherish. When you work, you are just like a flute through whose heart the

whispering of time turns to music. What is it to work with love? It is to weave the cloth with threads drawn from your heart as if your beloved were to wear that cloth. By a conscious effort you should train your mind to look for something bright instead of being morose. You should view your problems as challenges and opportunities to prove your mettle. You have to devise your own skills to tackle your

> ★ It is specific goals which take us where we want to go.

problems. You have to plan solutions based on your intellect and intuition. You should learn from the experiences of others rather than learn the hard way, that is to say, by making and repeating the mistakes made by you and others. You should divide your difficulties and problems into easily manageable segments. Then tackle each segment separately. Conceive all possible solutions for the problems and weigh the pros and cons of each. Do not hesitate to use your intuitive and reasoning power to decide the best possible solution. Always have a goal in front of you as it is the goals which keep you going. Keep up your momentum in fixing and achieving one goal after the other.

Develop yourself and grow up with your goals. Remember that nothing in life is achieved without a few setbacks and disappointments. Get back to your goals after doing mid-course corrections as all ships, missiles and rockets do. Goal-setting should be as essential as preparing the list of things to do or the shopping to be done. It is specific goals which take us where we want to go. Setting goals is the same thing as making a shopping list. One you make for your day-to-day living, the other you make to become what you want to become. Henry Ford used to say, "Whether you think you will succeed or not, you are right."

A successful man never imposes nor even dreams of limitations on himself by doubting whether he will succeed or not. A successful man looks at the problems facing him as opportunities to learn and to move forward. He makes a commitment to himself to do his best. On this subject it has been rightly commented by W. N. Mury, "Until one is committed there is hesitancy, the chance to draw back always, ineffectiveness concerning all acts of initiative and creation."

There is one elementary truth. Ignorance kills countless ideas and splendid plans. The moment one definitely commits himself then providence moves, too. All sorts of things occur to help one that would otherwise never have occurred. A whole stream of events issues from the decision rising in one's favour. All manner of unforeseen incidents, meetings and material assistance which no man could have dreamt of then come your way. A successful person knows that only when he is serious and committed will he achieve his objective. The very fact of desire to achieve unlocks his genius and energy to achieve his definite main aim. It is only the decision to achieve which leads to achievement. He does whatever it takes to achieve. To be successful you should enjoy whatever you are doing or have set your mind to achieve. Doing well is a reward in itself. Learn to work for the love of work and get involved. The only road to success is through clear and unambiguous purpose. The Gita says that you have the right to work but for the sake of work only. You have no right to the fruits of the work. Desire for the fruits of work must never be your motive in working. Never give way to laziness either. A successful man is generally happy because he likes what he does. Failure hurts but it is more hurting when failure comes your way because you did not give your best. Things improve when we ourselves improve. There is no magic wand to make things and circumstances better. It is a fact of life that despite

★ "Genius is one percent inspiration and ninety-nine percent perspiration. I never did anything worthwhile by an accident nor did any of my inventions come by accident. They came by work."

Thomas Edison

doing your best sometimes you cannot eliminate failure and disappointments. Doing your best itself is rewarding in boosting your own self-respect. You have to be persistent in your efforts to succeed. It has been rightly said that persistence is at the back of success. Calvin Coolidge said:

"Nothing in the world can take the place of persistence.

Talent will not. Nothing is more common than unsuccessful men with talent.

Genius will not. Unrewarded genius is almost a proverb.

Education will not. The world is full of educated derelicts.

Persistence and determination alone are omnipotent. The slogan: 'Press on' has solved and always will solve the problems of the human race."

Persistence is the main input for success and winning anything that one undertakes. Thomas Edison, the inventor of bulb and the gramophone, said, "Genius is one percent inspiration and ninety-nine percent perspiration. I never did anything worthwhile by an accident nor did any of my inventions come by accident. They came by work." Another great achiever said, "If people knew how hard I have worked it would not seem wonderful at all." "A man with half a volition goes backwards and forwards and makes no way on the smoothest road; a man with a whole volition advances on the roughest and will reach his purpose even if there be little wisdom in it. The man without a purpose is like a ship without a rudder, a waif, a nothing, no man. Have a purpose in life and having it throw such strength of mind, muscle into your work as God has given you," says Carlyle. A firm purpose is at least half-equal to the deed itself. Success lies in the constancy of purpose.

For joy, happiness and success the best way is to have a small baggage of needs, moderate expectations coupled with high aspirations and ambitions. Inaction should never be allowed to dominate your intellect. If you do so, it is almost like iron which rusts due to disuse. Aristotle said, "Moral excellence comes about as a result of habit. We become just by doing just acts, temperate by doing temperate acts, brave by doing brave acts." You may learn about the past but do not wallow in it. One way to be happy and successful is to get a job you love doing. Alternatively love whatever job you are to do. You should never feel that you are just working in your job. You should enjoy doing it. To be a success you have to take charge of decision-making at whatever level you are working no matter how painful that may be. Feelings should not matter. Says W.M. Thackeray: "The world is a looking glass and gives back to every man the reflection of his own face. Frown at it and it will in turn look sourly at you. Laugh at it and with it and it is a jolly kind companion." Every man has some quality which is unique in him. We can always learn something from every man. That man is most happy and infuses his life with joy who thinks creatively with new and interesting thoughts. There is everything in this life and world to make you happy. The only condition is that you yourself must be willing to accept it.

Planning Is The Key

Depending upon the position one occupies in a workplace there will always be people wanting to meet you for quicker disposal of work, for paying homage or for seeking clarification. At work, it is desirable to have some fixed time or hours for visitors. There will always be unscheduled and unexpected visitors who drop in beyond the scheduled timing. If you are a boss, it is best to notify some guidelines about what matters and for whom you will be willing to interrupt your work for and whom you will meet later on.

Before seeing an unexpected visitor, get information regarding how much time the visitor will need. Do not hesitate to ask the time frame, for an unscheduled but an important meeting, so that you can fit it in your other schedule. As Director of the CBI, I had heavy demands on my time from officials, friends and political masters. There was no way I could say no to any demand on my time. I would calculate how much time a visitor would need. Most of them would ask for five or ten minutes. I would set apart one hour for meeting visitors close to my chambers, which included five small meeting rooms. The visitors would normally arrive a few minutes earlier for the appointment. They would be served tea, coffee or cold drinks. I would walk into the meeting room and put on my stop watch and tell a visitor that his time started then. Exactly at the end of the time requested I would get up to leave. If the visitor said that he had not finished what he wanted to, I would give him a few minutes more to listen to him. This would be apart from the written brief or request the visitors were requested to bring with them. I would ensure that if I had promised that the visitor would have some reply sent to his communication in seven days, he would have a reply personally signed by me. I avoided unscheduled interruptions. In some cases, I would delegate the tasks to be done but kept a tab on them so that my own credibility was not affected. Instead of asking the visitor to go out at the end of the interview, I would myself walk out of the room. This did not hurt the ego of the visitors as they were never asked to go away. Instead, I would get up and shake hands pleading that I had to see the next visitor. If at all I had to see somebody in my office room which was rare, then I would receive them at my office door and greet them. This would give me control over the length of the time I wanted to spend with them as they would already have been softened by my politeness. If some problem came to my notice, I would decide to handle it right there and then. Only if I could not completely handle it, would I plan to take care of it at a later time, but definitely, within the self-imposed time frame.

In government offices in India, senior executives let the visitors know that they are busy and are not to be disturbed by placing a red light, at the top of their door which is a kind of a 'Do not disturb' sign. Everybody has his or her reasons to be busy. He or she need not be afraid to say 'No' to people to protect his or her work time. One does not have to be apologetic or need an excuse to be too busy. When interruptions occur, use a system like a bookmark to remind you where you left. Have a definite system of jogging your memory so that it will be easier to pick up where you left off.

Save Time

If you are right-handed, put your phone on the left side of the desk so that you can hold the phone to your ear and take notes at the same time, if required. It is not necessary to answer the phone every time it rings, if you are busy with other urgent work or cannot take the call for some reason. Have a system where all such calls automatically go into the answering machine or into voice mail box. This is also one way to avoid interruptions. The message on your answering machine should be clear and to the point.

Let people know through your answering machine when you will return their calls. This will also enable you to filter your calls so that you can avoid unnecessary high pitched sales calls, irritating or crank calls. This is also a way to save time. My own method is to let every call go into the answering machine even if I am sitting next to the telephone. Only after the caller has identified himself and stated his purpose I respond if I feel that I should. I use the voice mail as a time saving tool.

Alternatively, you can tell people through the answering machine or the voice mail exactly what you need to know or how they should contact you and the best time to reach you. When leaving messages, ask the person who has received the call to repeat your message back to you to make sure he has got it right. If you are going to be out for a long time or the subject is dealt by somebody else you can also ask if some other person can help the caller. Give the name and contact number of the other person with his prior consent who can help the caller quickly. Respect your own time as well as other people's time. Collect all the information you need to take care of a request before returning any phone call.

Be Technology Savvy

The new technology which is available in the market is mind-boggling and can add tremendously to your office efficiency. Do not hesitate to learn to use all the functions of the phone like forwarding and retrieving calls, conferencing etc. Learn to use gadgets as effective instruments.

Prioritize For Productivity

The biggest problem I face in my work and life is prioritizing. Most people also face the challenge of their lives in deciding the kinds of activities and responsibilities they should take up, and what should be delegated. Normally all of us should enjoy doing what we are doing but we forget to pay attention to enjoy what we are doing. It is again a struggle to identify and to let go of the boring, tedious and time-consuming tasks that clutter and eat up our day. It is incredibly difficult for most people to confess that they cannot do everything themselves. Some activities and things to be done in our lives are outside our experience, competence, range of expertise and inclination. Some of them are unpleasant or just not what we want to spend time on. There is nothing wrong with admitting that we cannot or do not want to do a few things as long as we can find someone else to do them. The key is to create a successful 'Not-to-do' list. This can be done by paying attention to what you do, how long it takes, how often you do it and whether or not you get some benefit from that particular activity. However, because of habit most people spend a lot of their time on autopilot so that at the end of the day they cannot recall the amount of time spent on each activity. It will make matters easier if you keep a record of your daily activities. This will help you in identifying the things you do not want to do even if you had the time. This is the only way to creating a 'Not-to-do' list. This list can help you identify chores, errands, jobs and daily responsibilities that you feel you can and should delegate to other competent persons or people working for you.

> The key is to create a successful 'Not-to-do' list.

The best is to log everything and track your job or work activities filling your day including travelling time to and from your place of work or external responsibilities like committee meetings, socializing, visiting friends or going to clubs. This will enable you to spot areas where you can trim and tighten your schedule through delegation. Make a note of what you are doing. It may be checking e-mail, an idle visit to computer sites, cleaning the house or visiting the market for buying groceries or vegetables or other items. Estimate how much time you have spent on such chores or errands including travel, dressing, and preparation time. This is the beginning of the preparation of your 'Not-to-do' list. Also, calculate how much is your time and work worth? Many people do not value their time or know its worth in concrete financial terms. But unless you realize that your time is intrinsically invaluable you will never be able to decide how it is best spent. The following is a general guide you can use in determining how much an hour of your time is worth. One hour a day, well or poorly spent, adds up in the following way in one year's time:

Your Annual Income	What One Hour Is Worth	One Hour Per Day For A Year
Rs 25,000	Rs 12.61	Rs 3,125
Rs 40,000	Rs 20.49	Rs 5,000
Rs 50,000	Rs 25.61	Rs 6,250
Rs 75,000	Rs 38.42	Rs 9,375
Rs 1,00,000	Rs 51.23	Rs 12,500
Rs 1,25,000	Rs 65.10	Rs 15,884
Rs 1,50,000	Rs 76.84	Rs 18,750
Rs 1,75,000	Rs 89.65	Rs 21,875
Rs 2,00,000	Rs 102.46	Rs 25,000
Rs 2,50,000	Rs 128.07	Rs 31,250
Rs 3,00,000	Rs 153.69	Rs 37,500

* Based on 244 working days per year

You can examine delegating in terms of the biggest financial gains. When you have hired someone to take care of an item on your 'Not-to-do' list, calculate as to how much you are paying him and whether you are getting the best out of him. For example, for a person earning Rs. 400 per hour it is best to pay Rs. 13 per hour to someone you delegate for doing a routine job. I have my private secretary doing all the routine work and my driver to drive me around. They are selling me their time at a cheaper rate. I use my time ten times more per hour for doing more important work.

The same is true when I hire anybody else. For instance,

a computer mechanic will do a task in half an hour by giving the right commands that would take me four hours to complete through hit and trial methods. This enables me to focus on higher priority work without worrying about other chores.

Plan Before You Organize

You cannot create a truly useful space unless you have the final expected result in view. Ask yourself as to what you expect from your storage. Do you want to maximize it and be able to see everything you own? Do you want to protect your costly items and cut down the time spent on cleaning and dusting? Do you want to have something special about the room like displaying or concealing your stored items? Keep your objectives in mind as you organize your storage space. Your choice should be to determine as to what you want to accomplish with your organizing efforts. Everything what you do whether it is cleaning the house or buying anything should fit in within these goals.

What Is Holding You Back?

All of us want to get organized. The first thing in getting organized is to find our obstacles and conquer them. Make a beginning by conquering obstacles for starting in right earnest.

Sometimes the quest for perfectionism holds us back. We occasionally feel that we should start when we have enough time to do a job thoroughly. One way to tackle this kind of mindset is to choose smaller projects or parts of projects that can be completed within 15 minutes to one hour or less. It is important to keep yourself motivated. Approach your projects as something which are going to give you pleasure and fun. Reward yourself for all that you accomplish no matter how small they may be. Never hesitate to ask for help from a friend. Make all efforts to keep your motivation level high. You might feel overwhelmed because you are focusing on every trivial thing that needs to be got done.

Just choose one or two small projects to focus on at any given time. Grab your solutions and motivation from whichever source you can. Effective solutions solve the problems effectively.

How do you act or react to your life? When you are merely reacting to events in your life, you are putting yourself in a weak position. You are only waiting for things to happen in order to take the next step in your life. On the other hand when you are enthusiastic about your happiness you facilitate great things to happen. It is always better to act from a position of power. Never be a passive victim of life. Be someone who steers his life in exactly the direction he wants it to go. It is all upto you now.

> ★ Reward yourself for all that you accomplish no matter how small they may be.

Getting Organized

If you do what you have always done and in the way you have done it you shall get only such results which you have always got. Getting organized requires that not doing things that cause clutter, waste of time and hurt your chances adversely of realizing your goals. You should concentrate only on doing things that eliminate clutter, increase your productivity and provide the best chances for achieving your goals.

1. The first step should be to stop leaving papers and other things on tables, desks, counter tops and in all kinds of odd places. The more things you leave around in places other than their rightful places the quicker the clutter will accumulate. Keep things in their assigned places after you have finished using them. It does not take long to put something away. If you leave things lying around they will build into a mountain of clutter. It could take hours if not weeks or months to trace them and declutter the atmosphere.

2. Start writing the tasks to be done. If necessary, jot down important dates and events in your calendar or in the tasks list in the computer if you have one. Do not trust your memory but make written lists of tasks to be done and items to be remembered. It is best even to write your ideas on a piece of paper as they occur to you.

Remember if you try to keep everything in your head it is only going to make confusion worse confounded. It is incredibly easy to forget something important that needs to be done and mostly, important things get neglected if they are not written down. Another way is to speak the tasks to be done in a mini-cassette recorder and then transfer the same on to paper. I personally keep a pen and paper, pad or diary near my worktable. I carry a mini-cassette recorder in my pocket during my morning walks and keep the same next to my bed so that even if I remember something to be done even at odd hours or in the middle of the night I speak into the tape recorder and act on the ideas after getting up. I prefer not to use tiny scraps of papers, hotel napkins or empty cigarette boxes. Another technique I use is to write down the jobs or tasks to be done in a regular diary and tick off every job done. Sometimes when I am not at home I note down the work to be done in my electronic organizer which has a memory of 512 KBs, but my first preference is still to write down everything in a diary for easy follow-up.

There is a good chance that tiny scraps of papers will make their way under a mountain of papers in my study room never to be found again when I might need them. I do not try to get a large number of things done at the same time as it would overwhelm me leading to a good chance that nothing substantial will be accomplished. I try to be realistic in determining the number of tasks I can complete in any given day. I have a list of long-term jobs to be done and the jobs to be done today along with the jobs to be done on a short-term basis. I do not neglect long-term jobs or short-term jobs and assign them the correct priority. I transfer a few long-term items to a few short-term jobs to be done so that care is taken of both long-term and short-term objectives. This way there is a good possibility of both being

> It is important to keep in mind that the measure of our success and happiness does not lie in the quality of the cards we are dealt by unseen hands but the poise and wisdom with which we use them and play them.

completed side by side. It is helpful to adopt this practice because sometimes there are not enough daily tasks to be done and so all the time can be devoted to long-term projects. Work is an ongoing activity and should be done on a day-to-day basis. My effort is to put neither too many or too few items on my 'To Do' list. I try to complete routine chores daily. If for some reason I am not able to accomplish everything the same day, then the following day I try to put fewer items on my 'To Do' list. If, however, I have completed everything with time to spare, I pull out a few more items from my long-term objectives on the list to use the spare time. I am never negative towards myself by condemning myself that I cannot get organized. A negative approach almost always results in failure. I encourage myself by saying that I can tackle my problems by taking one step at a time and being patient with myself. I find that with this approach I can accomplish almost everything. It is important to keep in mind that the measure of our success and happiness does not lie in the quality of the cards we are dealt by unseen hands but the poise and wisdom with which we use them and play them.

Norman Vincent Peale remarks, "The 'how' thinker gets problems solved effectively because he wastes no time with futile 'ifs' but goes right to work on the creative 'hows.'"

Marion Woodman adds, "Be focused on your goal by not letting yourself be distracted by the 'what ifs'. Often we distract ourselves on purpose by focusing on everything that can go wrong because we want to quit. When this happens, shift your focus to the 'how'. Focus on completing one step at a time one day at a time. Focus on how you are going to achieve your dream and not on whether or not you will achieve it. Immerse yourself in the details of your success so that you will not be distracted by the 'what ifs'. And in doing so make your dream a reality!"

All of us live and work within fixed patterns. These patterns and habits determine the quality of our life and the choices we make in life. There are a few vital things to know about ourselves. We should become aware of how much we influence others, how productive we are and what can help us to achieve our goals. It is important to create an environment which will promote our success. We should consciously create a system that would enable us to achieve our goals. Most of us live in systems which have come our way by an accident, circumstances or people we have met over a period time. Some people work in offices with outdated equipment. We are surrounded by our colleagues or subordinates who happened to be there by the fact of sheer recruitment earlier or later by the management. Our daily routines and schedules have been formed on the basis of convenience, coincidence, the expectations of society and sometimes due to superstitions. The trick for success is to have an environment that helps in attaining our goals. If you love music, then choose a tempo, rhythm and volume that will keep you humming and happy. Choose the colour which suits your mood in your office or your workplace.

> ★ Create and sustain a wonderful environment filled with beauty, peace, inspiration and hope.

When you want to concentrate keep the phone off the hook. Do the same during important meetings. Control your life. Make an effort to launch your day with a great start. A law of physics says that an object set in motion tends to remain in motion. It is the same thing with daily routine. To have a good start each morning will keep you upbeat during the day. If you begin the day stressed, you will tend to remain so that way. The best is to create a course of action or conditions where you are not hassled for being late for a meeting, worried about household affairs or distracted by happenings in the world. Aim to be highly successful. Control the direction of your life. Not only should you start the day on a cheerful note but also continue to do so during the day. Keep yourself stimulated and invigorated during the entire day. Start your day with a purpose. Have a daily direction and a trajectory of action. It will keep you on your course all day long. Throughout the day reinforce your positive values and your choices. Anything that helps you in maintaining your highest values and your most important priorities should be welcome. Be in control of your life and work. Create and sustain a wonderful environment filled with beauty, peace, inspiration and hope. Do not drift and let no interruptions including the telephone run your life.

Plan your day in such a way that suits your plans, objectives and makes you feel just right with the right amount of encouragement during the entire day. You should give a direction to your day and timing. Sort out your piles of papers, clear out your drawers, cupboards and car boxes from time to time. Get a box or a bag. Make piles. Label them as Throwaway or Giftaway. In the Throwaway pile keep all items which you do not know to whom they belong or are either outdated, beyond repair or not required. If it is a paper, a book or a file that you do not need or are not going to read then give it away. In India even the gift of an old or a dated book is welcome. As such it comes in the category of Throwaway or Giftaway. It should be thrown away or gifted to make place for something new and better. The point to keep in mind is to get rid of things you do not need or want. Store only what is current stuff or the things you need for reference and personal life mementos. Act promptly for anything which requires immediate action like making a phone call.

Enter all the information related to your job, family connections or friends into your planner, calendar or computer or any other place where you can retrieve it promptly. Be ruthless, determined and honest in your efforts to clear out the clutter within a fixed time schedule. Do not allow this decluttered space to be cluttered again. Reward yourself for the job. Draw up a plan of action for the things you want to delete from you life. Do not let the same material enter your life in some other form as referred, recycled, repaired or required to be stored. Bring a smile into your life by feeling relaxed and free of the junk.

Quick Methods Of Success

Most people are happy and comfortable in discharging their functions the way they have been used to working. They even resist minor changes in their working style and practices. Sometimes changes will gain not only appreciation of the superiors but will also improve personal efficiency. A few suggestions for better working are given below. Always make a plan of action of whatever you are to do during the day. Never start the day until you have listed the work and the things

> Think twice before making a commitment to anybody. Once it is made stick to it at all costs.

to be done. Make a habit to regularly outline such a plan. Post it prominently where it will always get your attention. If you are a manager, discuss it with your team for maximum achievement depending upon the individual or team job. Make the people working with or under you aware of the objectives and the mission of the organization as well as the targets set by the management. Show interest in knowing and implementing all goals. Remember that your survival and that of your organization depends on achieving set goals. It is important to know the expectations of the top management from you and your team or of the department handled or headed by you. It is best to form the habit of setting deadlines with a clear time frame for each target. No matter how trivial or big a target may be, finish it or have it finished in time. Inculcate in your team members the habit of setting and meeting deadlines. This will both improve your efficiency and develop confidence as well.

Always value, uphold and cherish your commitments. Think twice before making a commitment to anybody. Once it is made stick to it at all costs. It is not only your individual commitment. It is the commitment of the organization you work for. It is useful to do periodical self-evaluation. It is not necessary to go for any structured mechanism for self-evaluation. You can always design one for yourself. Your own review of yourself will ultimately be the best thing that can happen to you. Rate your performance yourself. Strive to excel your own record. There is no end to achievement or learning. Strive for perfection. Base your progress on your own self-evaluation score and the feedback you get from your bosses and colleagues. Identify the areas where you can do still better. Try hard to develop your skills in those directions.

Never be reluctant or ashamed to ask for aid. All of us need help from time to time. It is an interdependent world. The one who is asked for help will feel glad and honoured that he has been asked to help. Chances are that he will do his best to help you. Helping each other is the basis of all human developments, interpersonal relations and industry and commerce. Try it. It may help you to perform better. Always keep on planning and developing new ideas of doing better and more efficiently. Sharing ideas helps in straightening out irregularities and rough edges. Do not be afraid of any ridicule. It is ideas that move the world. It is ideas which have transformed civilizations.

Become the master of your profession or whatever job you are doing. Develop expertise and master your job. At the same time strive to get exposure in other fields related to your profession This will enhance your skills. Telephone calls sometimes have a habit of disturbing at peak working hours or when you just do not want any interruptions. You may use your voice mail or answering machine for recording such messages. Tell your friends and relatives the best time to call you. Receive and return your calls during your unproductive or lean hours. I use an answering machine. I have noticed that at least thirty percent calls are blank calls or wrong numbers. Undertaking too many jobs is sometimes the result of poor planning. People who plan many things at the same time end up not completing or doing any job well. Always prioritize your work to find out 'which is more important or urgent'. Important tasks should always be undertaken first followed by not-so-urgent work.

Unplanned meetings are both unproductive and a waste

of time. Always schedule your meetings with sufficient notice. They should rarely come as a surprise. Too many meetings or meetings for trivial issues or reasons and decisions only show that there is something wrong or unsatisfactory happening in an organization. Plan your weekly, fortnightly, monthly or quarterly meetings with an agenda, a list of participants and other details in advance. This will also enable people to confirm their attending the meeting. This approach will make the meetings more fruitful.

Employees at different levels come in all shapes, sizes and hues. Everybody has his or her own methods of working. They may be authoritarian or require reassurance, support and agreement for doing everything. Others can be complainers, critics, rebels, fighters and activists. Some employees say, "I am not paid for this so why should I do it because this not my job." Others are passing-the-buck type, mudslingers, and benign and not so benign saboteurs. The types mentioned above have more than one of those traits. Even adverse traits can overlap and they do so. Such people make it easier for the management to segregate good employees. The trick lies in using everybody for the work he or she is best suited for. There is some good and some talent even in the worst of persons. But a good employee who takes initiative stands heads and shoulders above others. Be an employee who does things on his own. He does not need

> Nobody should believe that their pay is their birthright whether they work or not.

a boss to tell him what to do. Do not be one who acts only when told exactly what to do. Even then he performs poorly. Be a person who does any assigned task well and cheerfully.

Be also cheerful when helping others and never sit idle. Always keep your commitments. Try to make life easier for your colleagues, subordinates and seniors. Any organization will want such a person. Never be afraid of accepting responsibility. Do not give any excuse whether genuine or otherwise to avoid additional responsibilities. When good workers are given a task, they do a good job and see it through to completion. Good employees are responsible for their own actions as well as their overall performance. All organizations engaged in commerce, industry or business are there to make money from their business. All their activity is focused on profits and performance. The pay cheques of employees are directly related to their organizations and businesses making money. Nobody should believe that their pay is their birthright whether they work or not. They should not think for a moment that it is the headache of their bosses to bother as to how their salaries are paid to them.

Nobody wants to work with a person who is complaining or grumbling all the time. Keep on doing consistently what is best for your organization. Never believe in doing the least and the easiest. Instead go in for giving your best. What is important is the overall performance and not scoring points. Be always disciplined. Stay on the right track by being a consistent performer. Earn the reputation of somebody who does all the tasks assigned in time and of one on whom the bosses can depend. Always keep your motivation high. Be a self-motivator. Even in the leanest of times where there is nothing much to be done find something useful to fill the time. Spend time learning something new that will help improve your performance. Always be on the look out for giving credit to others or your team. Aim to exceed expectations. Do more than asked for. Also, do a better job than expected. Do more than you are paid for. You will invariably be paid more for what you do.

You are a part and parcel of the organization you are working for. There is no such thing as 'they' or 'these people'. You are in the organization for some duty, assignment or a purpose. You have a responsibility for the functioning of the organization in your sphere of work. Participate actively in developing the systems which can take you and your organization places. If you notice drawbacks, devise remedies to change

> Centre your world around people who are friendly, tactful, cheerful, and fun loving.

them. It does not serve any purpose to curse your organization for in some way you are cursing yourself. Your endeavour should be to make your organization the best and at the top. Make yourself its best functionary. One way is to put order in your life and in your office. In a disorganized work area, important papers can be lost or misplaced. This invariably results in loss of time and energy. A shabby working place gives the impression that the person working there must also be shabby. It becomes difficult to dispel such impressions later on. Such impressions get carried to the bosses who matter. Be the best and give your best.

Be an original thinker with a vision. Always seek constant improvements in your methods of working and performance. Do not be afraid of difficult problems. Concentrate on them. Delegate routine jobs which more often than not are a waste of time. Centre your world around people who are friendly, tactful, cheerful, and fun loving. Such persons are generally sensitive and aware of others' feelings, good judges of men and deliver what they promise. They achieve goals without creating friction. They are generally practical and able to get good deals. They base their decisions on concrete facts. They have their own ways of realizing ambitious plans based on realistic perceptions of the prevailing situations. They may take expert opinions or consider management theories but they do not bind themselves to bookish knowledge. They cope with troublesome situations, difficulties and problems as they arise.

Original thinkers use various faculties like hearing, tasting, intuitive thinking and feeling in the quest of success. They keep the lines of effective communication open with different people at different levels. They use different strategies for different people and different work relationships. If even an ordinary person learns to communicate effectively, then even the biggest roadblock cannot stop him from succeeding. For those who fail in communicating efficiently, effectively and correctly there is hardly any chance for making a mark in life.

The Buffet Syndrome:
Too Much On Your Plate

Life is like a buffet offering a variety of choices every day and still having a lot left and enough for everyone to have. But everything has a price tag. For instance, to be fit we have to maintain a proper balance of vitamins, minerals, proteins, carbohydrates, fats and fibres. The same is true of all our activities and responsibilities. If we undertake too many projects, we will find it difficult to handle all of them.

Overreaching can create a lot of health and self-image problems for us. If we do not maintain a proper balance of our activities to take care of our physical, mental, spiritual and social needs, we create stress, disharmony, unhappiness and eventually dysfunction in our lives. Many of us including myself have still not fully mastered the fine art of saying 'No'!

Organizing life will enable us to focus on things that are really important and for which we feel that we do not have time. This approach will also enable us to have more time to relax and create time do the things which we enjoy doing. Other benefits include making more money, being punctual and spending more time on really important things which require attention. A good record-keeping is the first step in getting organized.

The real key to success is to concentrate on what matters most to us in our lives. It also includes restricting the number of jobs we undertake at any given time or on any given day and concentrating on the most important ones. Focus is the most important thing in life. Focusing on absolutely essential items and doing away with unimportant or not immediately relevant items is the best way to achieve success, health, happiness and our personal well-being. Create a list of the items that matter most to you. It should include work, contacts, people, both in the family as well as in the place of work. This list should be almost a sacred list. It should be prepared by spending all the time with wholehearted enthusiasm and passion. Be passionate about what you do. Find out what is sapping your strength. Is it because you are trying to win a popularity contest by trying to please everyone, or trying to be liked by everyone or trying to be a star or the saviour for all or trying to do everything perfectly or by saying 'Yes' to everything and everyone?

Identify the factors which are causing the over-commitment at the cost of things that matter to you most. Take at least one decision to consciously drop one inhibition which is holding you back. Doing your best is the next best thing to perfection. Perfection is not required for everything in life as absolute perfection exists only on paper or in fiction.

Check Your Self-talk

It is best to guard against words like 'should' or 'got to do' or 'have to'. Replace such words with 'may be', 'possible' or 'choose'. Each one of us can sit in the driver's seat for his life. If you do not want to do something which might be against your overall interests or against your better judgement, just do not do it.

Self-Reflection

Schedule some time for a day's retreat all by yourself to reflect on your successes and disappointments. This could be done every six months or once a year. This could be used for the current year to assess your wishes and targets as well as for the next year. Put down your responses to these questions as you reflect so that a record is available. Assess for yourself as to what worked

> ★ Simply making a resolution or wishing to achieve something does not lead to any achievement.

and moved you forward towards your goals and successes and what did not work and what discouraged you from moving forward? Learn the lessons from your experience and assessment. Apply them in the future to achieve your absolute 'Do' list. List the six most important areas in your life that need your attention and which are vital for you.

Every year most people make different resolutions to lose weight, save money and get better organized. These kinds of goals unless followed systematically become a ritual and are repeated mechanically from year to year with a poor success rate. Simply making a resolution or wishing to achieve something does not lead to any achievement. Achievement requires a resolve, intention, planning and action. Do not have a long list of unachievable goals. Creating and starting with a shorter, realistic and practical list needs all your skill, patience and your time. It is important to remember the old saying: "Rome was not built in a day."

Cost Of Procrastination

For several months now I have been postponing even telephoning my bank to check whether my pension is being credited at higher dearness allowance rates as sometimes the government circulars take a while to reach the banks before the pension amount is increased. The result was that I lost some money which could have come to my account at higher interest charges. Thus, procrastination is not only expensive but also a losing proposition. All it would have taken was a phone call to sort out the matters. I believe that all of us tend to postpone things we should be attending to immediately. What is required is a strong will to sort out these matters instantly. In terms of time, it does not cost much. It may hardly take a minute or two. The trick is not just to have good intentions but just do whatever is required to be done. Do not wait for the so-called 'right' moment. Do not feel uncomfortable with the idea of change and do not use it as an excuse for postponing prompt action. Do not justify delay on the grounds that you are waiting to feel more comfortable with the idea of change. Inaction is bound to create unhappiness. Do not allow doubts to gain a stranglehold on you and your self-confidence. This will make it easy to avoid putting off taking the next step.

Stop resisting change which in any case is inevitable. You cannot permanently avoid becoming more of what or who you are Confront your fears and overcome them. Try to find out as to what makes you afraid of change whether it is in your relationship with other people and their expectations or your disappointments? Then face and rationalize the change and subsequently address the issue or issues. It has to be recognized that all relationships must grow and that you should always strive to live up to your own self-esteem and expectations. If you do not do so, you are only guaranteeing unhappiness for yourself. You will be more disappointed if you do not make the attempt. It must be borne in mind that change is an opportunity to grow so do not be afraid of it. Never be afraid to challenge old ideas of what you can and cannot do. The opportunity to stop procrastinating and taking action on your goals is there right now. The only requirement is you should be willing to spot and take

> ★ Fear thrives and operates to the maximum extent in ignorance and the darkness of the mind.

advantage of it. Lamenting and regretting never helps. There will never be perfect conditions or time for all the things you want to do. You have to shape your life around your own goals by examining your habits and schedule. Determine the best time for your work and work consistently. You have to create a perfect programme for yourself by being flexible and realistic. If you are not a morning person, do not promise yourself a morning schedule.

It is a fact that the definition of perfectionism varies from person to person and place to place. There never were and there never will be perfect circumstances. It is futile to wait for them before starting to achieve your goal. Instead get started and create the right circumstances. It is the right self-motivation which can fuel your enthusiasm and make you start working towards attaining your goal. Sometimes you can be inhibited by an external obstacle. The logical answer for this problem is to come up with solutions that can put you on the trail towards your goal again. All of us have faced the prospectus of temporary derailment of our goals. Never allow your courage to desert you. The only solution is to confront your fears. Isolate your fears and determine as to what you are afraid of. Imagine the worst that can happen in case any fear does have a concrete expression.

Then visualize as to what you can do to improve the situation. Keep in view the best scenario and work out ways to attain it. Prepare yourself both for success and failure. Both have their own consequences. Both have the built-in scope for tackling situations and putting the ball back in your court. Fear thrives and operates to the maximum extent in ignorance and the darkness of the mind. However, if you have a clear idea of what you want to do next then you do not have to be afraid any longer. You have a choice and you should choose not to be paralyzed by any fear. You should use it as a stepping-stone to success and work through it.

It is the little things in life really which add up to make a complete whole. Do not put off what may seem a trivial matter in your life. A stitch in time can save nine. Any delay can take a heavy toll of your happiness. Little things occupy and clutter up space on the mental 'Do' list and affect motivation. After sometime there is so much trivia to be taken care of that you can feel demoralized. You do not know where to start. A stage comes when one feels that it is counter-productive to start at all. All this is the result of leaving small things undone and waiting for the 'right' moment to do them. It often means that we do not get them done at all. It is upto each one of us to create the right moment in our life. Life goes on and the right moment is the moment when we can make room for a positive change and take time to make our dreams come true. Undoubtedly, all this takes time. Nothing ever gets done unless one makes an effort to do it, so stop procrastinating. Stop wasting the opportunity for happiness that is available in the present moment. Stop putting off things. Do whatever needs to be done right now.

We need not look very far to see change happening in every aspect of our lives. In government, politics, democracy, industry and commerce change continues to occur all over the world. For example in technology, PC processors are available with an astounding speed of above 1GHz. In business, Fortune 500 companies announced 66000 job cuts in January 2001 alone. The rate of failed marriages has more than doubled from the early 1960s to the present. In western countries almost half of all marriages end in divorce. Change is inevitable in all spheres of life. The idea that 'the only constant is change' is not something new. It has been there for the last 5000 years. The only questions to be considered are 'how much?' and 'how fast'? Whether we like it or not all of us as well as the world are changing every moment. However, most of the time we resist change. Some people also feel that it is not necessary to change despite considerable evidence that almost everything in the world is changing. The idea of having to change ourselves or our environments as well as our friends is rather uncomfortable. Reactions to the very idea of the change vary from uncertainty, doubt, apprehension to a chilling fear. To avoid such feelings we prefer to retreat to the comfort zone of safety and security. Such feelings can render us powerless regarding the need to make certain decisions. It is the reason why most people remain as they are and where they are.

> Life goes on and the right moment is the moment when we can make room for a positive change and take time to make our dreams come true.

Change is essential both for growth and improvement. This is equally true in our own world or the limited world we live in as well as in our personal lives. Albert Einstein observed: "The significant problems we face cannot be solved by the same level of thinking that created them." It is true that all change is not improvement. But without change there will simply be no improvement so the question is how to face the process of change and embrace and create change in our lives which will empower us and bring about development and growth. Some suggestions are given below:

First of all, we have to understand that there is no real security that we get by remaining in our comfort zone. Security in the status quo is false. It is only living things that change and only through change we are truly alive. It is only by getting outside the comfort zone that one can take risks and achieve significant breakthroughs in life. Unless we become a change catalyst and proactive in our role as well as in aligning ourselves with the change agents in our world – technology, science and education we cannot achieve any great heights. Each one of us will have to create an action plan for the opportunities that come in our life. It is equally important to notice the outcomes and analyze the results of change. Change is a slow and subtle process. Change results from a series of small steps. Each step moves us closer to our desired outcome. Change is something which happens over a period of time. People who expect instant results may not even notice change for a considerable time. To live in harmony one has to learn to adapt. One should learn to adapt as the needs arise. In times of drastic changes, it is the adapters who rise to the occasion. While it is not possible to change the direction of the wind you can certainly change the direction of the sails of your ship. Stay on course. The wind will move you in the direction of your destination. Change will occur whether you like it or not or approve of it not. It is better to make a choice today to change for success. A successful change is called growth. It is never too late to change for a life of harmony. Why not start from today?

Clear Clutter Out Of Life

We are all victims of clutter. Overcoming clutter requires vigilance and constant watch otherwise it will overwhelm us. The list of clutter is endless and includes fused light bulbs, burnt-out plugs and sockets, empty bottles we hope to use, old magazines, old towels, broken utensils, dresses and outfits worn twenty years ago thinking that we can fit into them again at 55. Clutter can also be in the form of pending matters like unreplied telephone calls, e-mails or other communications, the appointments not kept or broken promises. Clutter prevents us from doing the things we really should be doing. Clutter is everything we do not use or wear or need on the grounds that it may come handy one day. Inherited objects and unwelcome presents given to us for which we have either no use or no liking are also clutter. The mind has its own clutter in the form of our own perceptions and past experiences which bind us to one particular state of mind. It is this clutter of the mind which makes us doubt our own abilities. This leads to our hanging on to situations and ideas which cause stagnation and do not let us move on. Most people hang on to a job thinking that they are indispensable or justify holding on to it out of a false sense of loyalty. The truth is that they are afraid to leap into the future and change direction.

It is the clutter of fear of the unknown which keeps people in a relationship. The fear of emotional upheaval is clutter which keeps most people unhappy. It is the cluttered approach which prevents people from not accepting a better job away from a familiar environment. These attitudes clutter our thought process. Physical clutter can be thrown away. A similar approach of letting go can only help us to clear out the mental clutter which restricts our development.

★ • • • • • • • • • • • •
• Clutter can also be
•   in the form of
•   pending matters
•   like unreplied
•   telephone calls,
•   e-mails or other
•   communications,
•   the appointments
• not kept or broken
•   promises.
• • • • • • • • • • • • • •

The major clutter problem in most homes is never or rarely used kitchen gadgets, empty gift boxes, gift wrapping paper, mementos or presents which are neither useful nor decorative. Home clutter also includes children's textbooks, old letters, broken boxes, assortment of keys, old tyres and tubes, broken brushes, empty bottles, packing material and a plethora of other sundry items. We do not need such clutter in our lives; yet most of us are not willing to part with the junk nor give it away in charity or sell it to raddiwallas.

Most of us hold on to old shoes and clothes on the ground that we might need them or fit into them or our children might use them one day. It is far better to live for today. It is best to create space for ourselves than to hold on to junk. Read and unread books and unlikely to read books occupy a lot of space in most houses. People do not get rid of them on the ground that it gives an impression to the visitors that the owner is a person of taste and learning. Some people consider it sacrilegious to throw away any book. Some which remain untouched and gather dust for years on end constitute a clutter. The world is moving and changing fast. Information unless it is history or science becomes out-dated almost before it is printed. Any information is available at the click of a mouse on a number of internet sites but somehow most of us including myself still like to hang on to old magazines and newspapers which also clutter up space.

The big question arises as to where and how to begin this fight. It is difficult to solve a tough problem or give up a long held habit at one go. Most of us do not have the heart to throw out the entire clutter all at once. Never attempt to rid the whole house of clutter at one go. If you do so you will start justifying to yourself for retaining everything as I do quite often. Always start in a small way. It may be one cupboard or one box or one drawer. Complete the whole task of clearing out, tidying and getting rid of unwanted items from one place before doing the same for the next place or next box. First, throw away a whole lot of empty cartons. Sort your items categorywise, for example, what you want to give to charity or as presents or to sell to the *raddiwallah*. It is simply a question of time as to how soon you can get into the act of 'chucking things out' enthusiastically. When the clutter is cleared you will only wonder as to why you did not do it earlier. More space will give an idea of openness and less congestion. You will also get positive vibrations in a clutter free area. Uncluttering life is a constant job. It is not something which can be done once and forgotten. Otherwise the clutter will continue overtaking you.

Motivation For Change

Knowledge acquired from education should translate into actual behavioural changes. There is a need for motivation to make the necessary changes in our behaviour. Most people go on sticking to their present methods of working based on the logic that why bother switching over to a new method or methods when the present ones seems to be functioning more or less efficiently. What many do not realize is that the skills involved in effective habits are essentially the same which build character and personality. Thus not being innovative or changing with the times is bound to lead to mediocrity. Personal skills are closely connected to success in career and in building healthy, interpersonal relationships. The following skills can form successful and effective habits. First of all, all methods require a readiness to accept a certain discipline. The skill to be developed is to devote time to your work everyday as well as in studying methods of better performance no matter whatever temptations or attractions may be there to claim your attention. The method of daily effort may have no immediate visible rewards but the pay-off comes at the end when the job or work is over. The pay-off is the result of persistence. Whatever anybody may say, there are no short cuts to success.

Invest and sustain an activity no matter how tedious it may be for the present. This is ultimately going to yield long-term rewards and benefits. Effective methods also involve decision-making skills as well as setting priorities for work after carefully weighing the pros and cons of your long-term and short-term goals. Also, time management is an important factor for all activities.

Unless you update your skills and competence you may be rendered redundant. You have to compete and match with the best. A new, more harmonious, forward-looking, development-oriented attitude is a charismatic factor. All-round good guys who can deliver the results will always be needed everywhere. The demand for constant improvement is going to stay for all times to come. It will also be the cause of many heads rolling with an unnerving frequency. Nothing can and should be taken for granted. Victorious executives battling and succeeding will always be in demand.

One might have a high-profile figure in one's personal life, interests, business or profession and generate a flattering image. However, the moment of truth, the hour of reckoning will surely arrive. The time of assessment of a sloppy performance always comes. The top person or persons and top

> ★ Personal skills are closely connected to success in career and in building healthy, interpersonal relationships.

management if they become stereotypes and not open to innovation can sink any organization. The style of performance of people vary. There are tough driving, no-nonsense leaders who know what they are doing when things are going downhill. In tough circumstances only the tough types rise to meet the challenges. While a tough man may not always have a nice guy image but he is admired for his grit and pulling through trying situations. It is better at all times to engage closely with the workforce. However, the switch in management styles from soft to hard can cause a sense of confusion in the workforces. Having been accustomed to one type of managers they need time to adjust to the new boss to deliver results.

This problem is not confined to any one particular sector either in the government or in the private sector in trading or in manufacturing. There can be a sense of alienation and confusion provoked by sudden changes. Confused or disenchanted workers cannot and do not invest any enthusiasm or energy in their work. In such circumstances the possibility is that most people will do their job in a low-key fashion just enough so that they do not lose it. Both their head and heart will not be in their work. It is better to take all possible steps to make sure that whatever promises are made do not turn out to be empty ones. Management style needs to be both charismatic and visionary and respond to changing situations. The workforce should not feel alienated by new methods of working.

Successful businesses and successful managers will always motivate their teams to refocus on the job at hand. They give them a feeling that they have an important part to play. Executive coaching is as important as re-training the workers and supervisors at middle and lower levels. Executives should be very clear about their roles. A mixture of toughness and carrying people along is still the ideal solution. There can be no universal model. It is bound to vary from time to time and situation to situation, but, basically, a clear management model will always have people who can meet all kinds of challenges and adopt different approaches. Cult leaders are few and far between. In any case they are a dwindling lot. Sometimes too much is expected of them. Fewer leaders who can manage their teams and network with each other is the only effective way of managing situations and workforces and getting best possible results.

Skills and taking pride in yourself positively will enable you to develop the quality of functioning independently. It will also earn the respect of your colleagues, bosses and subordinates.

Organising Events

Even in a comparatively poor and developing country like ours, celebrating weddings, birthdays, birth and death anniversaries of all sorts by the middle and poor classes of the population has become very common. Each such occasion is important to the person or persons in whose honour the celebration is being organized. In fact, many a time such an event is organized at the instance of the person who is being honoured or lionized. It is important for the organizers to decide on the type and the size of the celebration proposed. This decision is naturally determined by the size of the budget and financial consideration. Whatever be the occasion, whether big or small, some planning with the following guidelines will make the occasion memorable.

If the occasion or the cause of celebration is indicated in advance most guests turn up suitably dressed. However, it is for the host to decide whether any function is to be formal or informal. Advance intimation of such information saves the guests from any embarrassment as they know in advance as to what kind of dress is expected to be worn by them. It is useful to indicate the appropriate attire for the occasion by indicating whether the programme is formal or informal. For a formal function there are some clear-cut guidelines to follow. For government functions at the Rashtrapati Bhavan the guests are expected to be dressed formally. For informal functions the

> A combination of different backgrounds and people who can mix with each other goes a long way in making any party or an event successful.

host may indicate his preference Many personal and social events come in between the two extremes. It is for the host to decide as to how he wants to entertain and from what time to what time. Make it clear in the invitation that a particular celebration will last from say 8 pm to 10 pm or from 7 pm to 9 pm. Whenever any embassy gives a reception it indicates the duration of the function.

Guests

Selecting guests for different types of events is not easy. It is important to decide on the type of people to be invited for different occasions. For instance, for a child's birthday the most important group to be invited is the friends of the birthday child. For celebrating a wedding anniversary, say a fiftieth anniversary, the old surviving friends of the couple are a must as well as guests belonging to other generations. Good planning requires an appropriate guest list. This is an important first step in making the celebration of an event memorable. Guests should be appropriate to the occasion. They should not feel out of place. A combination of different backgrounds and people who can mix with each other goes a long way in making any party or an event successful. I have attended a number of parties where I felt out of sorts, as I could not vibe with the other guests. I put in an appearance only to show courtesy to the host. This kind of situation can be avoided by inviting an eclectic group of guests. The number of guests to be invited is dependent on the capacity and location of the place where the event is planned. I have seen in some weddings where the guests had to wait in a queue even for almost two hours to congratulate the couple. This only shows bad organization.

Numbers

It is vital that the place of the event should be sufficiently large to accommodate the number of guests. It often happens that location, budget, equipment and other factors are not kept in view when organizing any celebration or function.

Location

The location of the event is an important fact and this will depend on the season and weather. Whether the function or celebration should be at home, indoors or outdoors, hotel, country club, restaurant or in a specially set up facility are the several options you can choose from. Where you want to have your programme will depend on the mood of the celebration. The cost and number of guests will be the main factors in deciding the location.

Food And Drink

The menu for the function is something everyone remembers, especially, if it is inedible or delicious. The type of food served should have some relevance to the time of day, the event, location, type and number of guests. Most guests, in the evening, expect a drink and if you want to limit the timings of the service of the meals, it is best to indicate it. Always ensure there is enough food, and drinks, too, if you are serving them.

Invitation

The name of the host, the occasion, place, time, telephone number and address to RSVP should be included on all invitations. If the function is being held at a lesser-known place, then it is advisable to include with the invitation, a map showing the route to the venue. To remove any doubts, also include the type of dress to show whether the function is a formal or an informal one. If the function is not purely an entertainment or musical programme, then there should be some background music. The music can be recorded or a live band. It will depend on your budget and the occasion.

Looking Good And Feeling Great

Chaos and clutter can instantly drain us of our energy. It can put you in a foul mood. It can even lead to depression. The best place to start clearing your clutter is the bedroom, home, office as well as papers and files in your workplace. Many people would like to keep their drawing rooms spick and span as well as other places where visitors are received. However, visitors can come anytime. They do not come for inspection of the house to see how clean it is. It is good to have the entire house in the best possible shape. A clean and a neat place itself gives the appearance of a properly organized and well-run place. Organizing and cleaning your working area will make your spirits soar. It is vitally important to start decluttering and overhauling your

> ★ First, clear the clutter out of your mind and then from your surroundings.

living and working place where you spend more than one third of your life. Begin with the first room you see on getting up and the last room where you retire for the night i.e. your bedroom. This room sets the stage for your day and determines how you will feel, react and cope throughout your waking hours.

Start your day by listening to laughter, watching nature and the sunshine outside your window. Find an excuse to sing, whistle, hum or play music. It will lift your spirits and refresh you. Sing to yourself and wake up every morning with a smile on your face. Show the world all the affection and love in your heart.

Inhale and infuse yourself with fresh clean smells and scents around you. A scented candle, fresh flowers, scented soaps, lotions or oils give you a good feeling. They are definitely more encouraging than dirty smells or dirty clothes which overwhelm, depress or drain instead of rejuvenating and renewing you. It is important to renew, rejuvenate and elevate your spirits everyday. You can start your day with deep inhalation and stretching exercises, saying your daily prayers, reading a positive affirmation or doing meditation.

First, clear the clutter out of your mind and then from your surroundings. Plan the kind of surroundings you want to have around you as well as the kind of smells and ambience. A clear mind and a soaring spirit will make the course of your life smoother during the day. Each day renews life and the first one hour sets the tone for the day. The first few minutes are the formative minutes of everyday. Special care should be taken to begin your day well. It is a matter of individual choice whether you want to start your day with God, in peace or in attuning yourself. I, on my part, begin my day by reading inspiring prayers followed up by exercise. Some others start with meditation, prayers, yoga, walk in the woods, singing, aerobic dancing or engage in any activity that gives them a good and a cheerful start. Develop and establish your power centre. Draw on it for clarity, strength and love. Spend some time with yourself. Periodically close your eyes and remember the most pleasant scenes and happenings of your life. At the end of the day spend some time with the higher power, that is to say, your God, before sleeping. This practice will help build a more productive life.

This way you will breathe in the Universal positive energy and breathe out any negative vibrations. Develop your will-power for positive thinking and do not surrender to negative energy. Get rid of all the negative clutter and stuff in your surroundings and your life. Get rid of anything in life which appears a dead weight to you. Renounce anything which makes you feel sad or unhappy. Abandon anything that brings back sad and bad memories or makes you feel outdated. Discard anything that is broken and beyond repair, and things you will never use again or which will cost more to fix then replace. Jettison anything from your past which would embarrass your loved ones after you are no more or anything that does not mean the same to you any longer.

> ★ Develop your will-power for positive thinking and do not surrender to negative energy.

Decluttering should be done room by room, wall by wall, inch by inch, surface area by surface area. Just get rid of all the clutter you might have collected in one place. You will be amazed at the feeling of relaxation you get as well as the feeling of having achieved the impossible. Time invested in decluttering is time well-spent to have a paradise of your own. Always devote some fixed time to declutter. When you are decluttering that should be the priority, and not answering the telephone or watching TV. Stay focused on the job by not leaving the place till you have completed it or spent the time allotted for it. To ensure that you are not again faced with the same problem do not store or bring anything into the room you are decluttering that should not be there and does not belong there. Do not stock items which can be easily purchased. Decluttering habits should be carefully followed after you have decluttered. Utilize the rooms and the space in the house for specific functions. Your house should not become a junkyard.

Kalidas, a great Indian poet, pointed out the value of using our present to optimum benefit in the following words:

Look to this day!
For it is life the very life of life.
In its brief course
Lie all the verities and realities of
Your existence;
The bliss of growth;
The glory of action;
The splendour of achievement;
For yesterday is but a dream
And tomorrow is only a vision;
But today well lived makes every
Yesterday a dream of happiness
And every tomorrow a vision of hope.
Look well therefore to this day!

Be well-organized and keep all your important phone numbers, account numbers, contacts for home maintenance at one place. Also keep a record or an inventory of where you keep your most important documents. Keep them in a place where you can lay your hands on them easily. These items are the tools of all human relationships as well as the key to your efficiency. They must be kept handy.

Keep Your Closet Neat

I have been keeping both winter and summer clothes for the last thirty years. I still have a coat stitched in 1961 as part of the formal dress when I joined the National Academy of Administration, Mussoorie, for training as an Indian Police Service Officer. I have outgrown it and the coat has outlived its life but I still have not got rid of it. Similarly, I had clothes stitched for me when I was a teenager. I found one day that this old baggage was preventing me from wearing my new properly-fitting clothes. As a traditional Indian I did not want to give them away, partly from sentimental reasons and partly, because they were pretty expensive. However, one day I made a bundle of all such items and gave them to some poor people. If you ask me what I gave away I will not even be able to recall, as to what I gave away. Any clothes that you did not wear in the last one year because they did not fit, were out of style, or you did not feel comfortable or good wearing them, should be got rid of. I assure you that you will not even miss them. I try to follow a rule, I admit somewhat difficult, that for every one new set of clothes in, two must go out.

I also store my clothes and take them out for use, season-wise. It is best to store your clothes, according to the weather. The winter clothes are hung on a hanger and stored in an almirah used for storing off-season clothes. The seasonal clothes are kept in my daily use closets. If you do not have space, then you can store the off-season clothes in a different part of the house or in your store, if you have one.

Different clothes are required for different occasions. A formal occasion requires formal clothes. A dress for a marriage will be entirely different than a dress required for a casual occasion. However, the effort should be to be best dressed at all times as it is the clothes which identify a person, in the first instance. Different kinds of weather and timings of the same season require different clothes. A full-sleeved shirt should be worn with a suit and a tie. In summer normally a safari suit or half-sleeved shirts or bush-shirts are worn. It is upto each one of us to organize our clothing according to purpose and style (formal, casual, shirts, pants, short sleeve, long sleeve. Other categorization can include colours (light to dark) and the style.

If you are sharing a cupboard with your wife or sister, then you can further store and categorize clothing — men's / women's, pants / shirts — by assigning each type, to a different part of the closet and separating them with a rod divider or any other partition.

In my house, my wife keeps several baskets, for washing clothes, ironing, and drycleaning. It makes it easier for everybody in the family to know where what clothes should go. Due to change in season, sometimes, there are clothes which are not currently wearable. There are hooks or brackets in the closets apart from the horizontal or vertical racks. You can hang just about anything from them like purses, belts, ties, handbags. For storing your shoes, use a shoe rack which can be placed independently on the floor. I use a shoe rack with four different compartments for storing chappals, walking shoes, formal shoes and shoe accessories. Another type of shoe rack, is a built-in one at the bottom of the closet. Sometimes, a cloth shoe rack can be hung on the back of the door. The shoes in this kind of rack are equally protected, aired out, and visible. The size of the shoe rack required depends on the number of the shoes you possess or want to stock.

Some clothes not need not be hung like vests, underwear, handkerchiefs, or socks. You can keep them on open shelves, in bins or in a drawer depending on the type of cupboard you have.

Declutter Your Space And Your Life

Clearing out clutter is a constant need. Every possible opportunity should be utilized, to declutter. It is not a one-time exercise. It is best to have three containers, labelled: 1. To be Preserved. 2. To be Cleared Out. 3. Doubtful whether to preserve or get rid of. You can devise a litmus test, as to why you want to preserve any item. You can ask yourself the questions: Does it have an emotional value? Is it useful or too expensive or too beautiful to be given away? This should help you in deciding as to why you are hanging on to it. While cleaning out, you will come across items which need to be cleaned out, repaired and borrowed items which should be returned or items which can be gifted away. After you have finished this exercise, do not feel guilty about throwing out or giving away the rest of the items.

Use transparent, square (or rectangular) storage containers to avoid any possible guesswork as to what is where. Label all the containers so that you can easily access what you need. Proper stacking and storage makes it easier to see what is available in each box at one glance. One way of maximizing space is to instal additional shelves. You can use old empty boxes for storage rather than stacking too many containers one on top of the other. Ensure that in the process of decluttering you do not cause another clutter of furniture.

While storing containers, be careful about storing heavy, bulky, or hard-to-handle items, at great heights or on lightweight shelves. Heavy items should not be placed on light items as they will crush the latter. A falling heavy item may also cause injury. Climate is an important factor for storing items. The items should be stored in such a way that they are not damaged by heat, cold, moisture, termites or other insects. Unless the belongings are well protected, there is no point in spending hard-earned money on them.

Be Generous With The Use Of A Waste-paper Basket

Keeping a waste-paper basket or a dustbin near the spot you are working is a great incentive to immediately toss out anything that is out of date or has outlived its utility. Incoming paper which includes your mail or other papers should be dealt with on a daily basis. First, you should decide as to why and what you need to do with each letter or piece of paper that comes to your table. If you are a very busy person and are likely to forget what you have decided about each person, then make a written note on it in pencil as to how you want to dispose it off. If it is something which needs urgent attention, put a red sticker on it and flag it with the deadline for disposal. If it is in your power to dispose it off, do so straightaway after getting all the related papers. Flag any items that require immediate attention with a red sticker and/or put them into a folder marked 'Today or Urgent'.

Sort out your papers. Keep your folders also subjectwise. It will help to link the papers easily. For instance, I personally have a folder on income tax, another folder for my bills, and yet another folder to keep records of expenditure or other important papers. It makes it easy to link with the previous papers. I keep papers that require a decision or an action on my part, stored separately from items that are kept for reference purposes. I also set aside time periodically to go through my papers to take care of any pending action items that have accumulated. I also have a programme in my computer which reminds me as to what is to be done on a particular day in a month.

How To Have Enough Working Space

In our country unless you are the boss in an office, everybody else has to manage with limited space. A feeling of openness and spaciousness adds to efficiency and effective functioning. If there is a constraint of space and place, certain types of furniture like 'L' and 'U' shaped tables offer the most efficient work spaces. These tables or desks give you plenty of manoeuvring space. They also provide an easy access to all the gadgets you may want to place on your table, whether it is a computer monitor or a fax machine, a telephone or a laptap computer. For efficient working, keep everything you need within easy reach of your chair so that you do not have to bend, stretch, or trek across the room to get it. At the same time, do not use your table as a hoarding space for the items you may need. Keep only that what you need nearby and put the rest where you can retrieve it in times of need.

Sort out all your incoming papers, including mail, magazines, newspapers or any other type of correspondence daily. Decide on the disposal of each paper the first time you see it if you have the related papers. If it is something which cannot be disposed off immediately, then keep it in an appropriate folder. You can have a folder for bills to be paid or for letters to be replied. Have a filing system which enables you to have an easy access to the papers as well as a system of reminders. Every office, whether government or private, has a set system of filing but it is equally important to keep your personal papers, whether they pertain to insurance, (household, car, or life) or payment of taxes and other bills. Divide your folders in the categories 'to read', 'to pay', 'to file' and create logical sub-categories and alphabetize the same within each category. This will enable you to remember and recall. Have a system of putting up slips on folders indicating the next date of action.

Use only one type of engagement diary or a calendar and record all your engagements in it. If it is done regularly, there is no chance of your forgetting an important meeting or business and personal appointments.

Save Your Space

Do not waste your table space by using it as as space for hoarding supplies. Only keep what you need at hand and put the rest in storage or elsewhere in a nearby closet or a set of drawers. You can always keep paper clips, pins, letter openers, staplers, tape, glue, pen and pencils etc. in a drawer, tray or baskets. Keep folders, note pads, paper sheets, file covers in stacking trays or in a separate container. Similarly find a suitable container, or a drawer for storing greeting cards, small note pads, and envelopes. To avoid clutter follow the 8/10 rule, that is to say when you have finished 8/10 of the items, it is time to replenish and buy more. Keep a standard supply list of the items you use regularly. When you have almost exhausted the stock, check and replenish it.

Keep a reminder to remind you that when you have reached 8/10 of the supplies, it is time to buy more of that supply. If you have the space, buy your supplies in bulk. It will save both money and time. Have a system which will prevent your running, at the last minute, for supplies of small but useful items that you use.

Filing System Is The Key To Efficiency

Have a filing system with broad categories. For instance, your medical record can be divided into sub-categories, like " fever, operations, infectious diseases, water borne diseases" and further alphabetized in each category. Begin file folder headings with something you can understand like 2003-Articles which can be further divided into financial, political or good governance.

Create a proper file index so that it is easy to locate each category and folder when you need it. Some files which are required on day-to-day basis can be called fingertip files like phone directories, shopping catalogues and frequently used telephone numbers. These need to be kept in such a place that they can be accessed at any time. Clip multiple-page documents together with staples or a binder clip so that you can see each page separately.

Indicate the trash or the discard date on each file or the items therein which have become outdated. Weed out your files at least once in six months. You can have a system, if needed, to print 'drafts' on coloured paper and the final copy on white to avoid any confusion.

Create And Depend On 'To Do' List

Never keep your 'To Do' list in your head. Empty it on a piece of paper and keep this list nearby so that you can add extra items as and when the need arises or as they occur to you. Your daily task list should also include items like scheduled appointments and urgent items that have to be given the highest priority. Limit your daily 'To Do' list to no more than 7 items, which should be completed including one or two difficult tasks. Create a timetable for your daily task list. Schedule time for completing specific jobs whenever possible. Examine your daily 'To Do' list, to check whether each task is necessary and whether it has to be done by you or whether it can be delegated or simplified. Do not wait until the last minute to complete a task. Create artificial deadlines and motivate yourself to finish your tasks early.

Everybody has his or her work style or work rhythm. Some people like to work in short bursts, others in long stretches, early in the morning, or late at night. Different people have different high or low-energy periods. You should schedule your day and make your programme accordingly.

Liberally use memory joggers. Make a list of things to take with you when you go for shopping or for a meeting. A memory jogger can be an alarm clock, an alarm on your watch, or on your computer.

4

SUCCESSFUL MANAGEMENT

Managing Successfully

To become an effective and an efficient manager is neither as difficult as many think nor is it as hard to achieve as most people believe. You need the will and the drive to succeed. This is the only way in which any reasonably able executive can become a high-powered, high profile and a result-oriented manager. Such people will always have a high employability quotient. Anybody can do his best when he is feeling on the top of the world. The real litmus test of the ability is to deliver even in the face of adverse circumstances and low morale. In adverse moments it is easy to give in to the temptation of snarling at your colleagues or your subordinates or anybody you come in contact with or give an impression of doing them a favour even when it is your duty to do a particular job. Try to be a good role model. Set the standards when it comes to your personal deportment. Make certain that your standards are high.

A foolish indulgence or impulsive behaviour can ruin years of your efforts as far as your career and reputation are concerned. Exercise self-control. It means staying cool when handling fractious people. Never indulge in backbiting.

You should not try to prove that you are the boss by bullying everyone around. Perhaps you might have observed some persons using intimidation to get others to fall in line. Your success in your job and your efficiency largely depends on the support and assistance of others. Lone rangers are not always the most productive or the most efficient. If you are a vicious weight-thrower you are likely to get only grudging, half-hearted co-operation from your colleagues. Mistreatment of your fellow workers will also affect your own self-esteem adversely. This is because though you may feel high after humiliating others you will feel sorry for having done so later on. You will feel lonely and isolated. In this kind of situation if you do not perform effectively you have only yourself to blame.

Be A Role Model

A role model leader or a manager should cash in on the advantages of his own courteous behaviour. Extend little courtesies like opening the door for visitors and others. Courtesy oils the hinges of relationships. Do not consider time spent with your staff as wasted time. It is ultimately teamwork which produces results. Imagine while on a flight you hear over the public address system, "Ladies and gentlemen I have good news and bad news. The bad news is we have been hijacked and are on our way to Lahore. The good news is that we are twenty-five minutes ahead of schedule." The bad news certainly outweighs the good. It is almost the same with your career. You need definite and clear-cut goals. If your goals are unclear, your career path will be both messy and uncomfortable and you will be spending most of your time running very hard to stay in the same place. Effective leaders to remain effective must set goals for themselves and their organization. The people who work for effective leaders expect it from them. Most subordinates feel let down when there are no clear goals set for them. One way to circumvent this problem is to write down your goals. Also, let the people or leaders you are working with or for know them. Post goals prominently for all to see. This way you can constantly remind others and yourself of them. This will also keep the goals in sight at all times.

> ★ Your success in your job and your efficiency largely depends on the support and assistance of others.

Criticism, however constructive, is never pleasant or welcome. However, a fair and an accurate criticism provides you with almost a clear picture of the shape of things to come. Never be perceived as hostile to any feedback. If you do so, people will hesitate in telling you the truth and what you need to know for achieving your goals. Consequently, you, your methods and your effectiveness will suffer both instantly and in the long run. There is nothing you can do about it. Your subordinates and your peers are often the best source of such inputs. Listen to them carefully and then act for any correction which may be required.

Problem Pundits Should Be Out
. . . .

You do not require much expertise to pick holes in something and point out mistakes. Problem pundits take delight in finding faults. Such people are there in every office and every workplace. These are the people whose careers have come to a standstill. They have been relegated to the back stage for unsatisfactory performance. They are prophets of gloom and doom. For them every problem assumes frightening proportions. It is better not to take their counsel. Instead, you should do your best. Do not blame the boss or the top management for your poor performance. It shows your weakness and disloyalty. It is a poor example to your subordinates who will make the same assessment about you. You should support the objectives of the management and your own organization even if you do not agree with them. The best course would be to make constructive and relevant suggestions. It will show your sincerity and dedication. Become a sheikh who provides solutions rather than alibis. However, if you still feel the need to express your personal views then do so with well thought-out arguments. Whatever the decision of the organization regarding the course of action, you should be equally enthusiastic in giving your best.

Managing Bosses Delicately
. . . .

Superiors feel that they have superior and more knowledge of everything than the people working with or under them. When presenting a solution to a problem to the boss, it is important to word it properly. What you want to say may be said in a manner which does not indicate an attitude of disdain or superiority. The formulation should be carefully thought out. Presentation needs to be formulated and presented in a manner that does not smack of any insolence or superiority but a support to the boss. It should appear as something which the boss had thought of and planned earlier.

No superior likes to be given an impression that his subordinates àre more intelligent than him or be told what is to be done. Bosses all over the world feel that they are the repository of all wisdom in the world. Some bosses do not like a subordinate

> ★ No two people react to the same situation alike.

getting credit for a job. Most bosses also do not like to concede that a subordinate possesses more knowledge on any subject than him. Showing off knowledge or expertise by a subordinate is a cardinal sin in the eyes of most bosses. Bosses are both mercurial and temperamental. They want to know all the time what is going on in the organization. By-passing or taking unilateral decisions and superimposing unsolicited ideas on the boss can lead to unpleasantness and problems. Appropriate and delicate strategies for volunteering tasks, making suggestions, overseeing arrangements, supporting, assisting, providing requisite back-up information, careful accounting and regular reporting to the boss are a must.

Dealing With Subordinates

Human relationships are a complex affair. No two people react to the same situation alike. Sometimes a situation arises when a subordinate does not perform his job properly, especially if a deadline has to be met. This can at times ruin the overall goals of the organization and is determental to the entire team's output. Different strategies are required for dealing with different subordinates with different levels of intelligence. It can involve repeated summarizing, requesting, gentle persuading, explaining and facilitating. "He or she works with me" instead of "He or she is my subordinate or a secretary" works wonders in treating people appropriately and with respect. Giving an impression of equality in relationships flatters the ego of the juniors. At the same time when dealing with subordinates a chain of line of command or a bottom-line and a respectable distance needs to be maintained. The subordinate should know clearly as to what extent he or she can poach on your personal or social territory The clear line of toleration lays down the limits for everybody.

Dealing With Colleagues

With colleagues a different kind of communication at a horizontal level is required. It includes making requests, sharing information, confirming, reassuring, assisting, and providing explanations and a mutual 'give-and-take' approach. This is an entirely different situation where you are asking for a favour or help from a colleague who may not be a boss but may still help you in your quest for excellence. It is a delicate situation where sometimes some colleagues may not relish the idea of pushing your career upwards.

Never Blame The Management

In our country whenever anything goes wrong or is done wrong the usual approach is to blame the establishment or the government. If a bus driver is rash or the buses do not run on time, there is increase in the population, a school does not admit a child, your neighbour spreads dirt around your house, shopkeepers overcharge you or servants commit theft, the fall guy is the government.

This holds true of the middle and poor classes. Even in private offices the in-house government called the management gets flak for all failures. Management is about 'managing men tactfully'. The fact is that sometimes the management is quite helpless in many situations. It may be more so where it might have run out of tactics about how to deal with the ever-increasing battery of non-performing manpower.

Incapacity, lack of competence, inadequate vision, insufficient motivation and insensitive management are some of the root causes of all the ills which result in low levels of productivity. The staff in this kind of climate continues performing in the same way as they were doing initially.

Many managements claim that people are their most important assets. But every asset requires a routine maintenance schedule. What should the management do about it? Companies the world over are going out of their way to keep their employees happy and contented. But the employees also have to realize that they swim or sink with their employers or organizations. Blaming the management all the time is not justified. If companies flourish, so will the employees. Both swim or sink together and both are partners in success and failure as the goal of both should, ideally speaking, be the same.

Be A Change Leader
. . . .

The only constant factor in life and the world is change. It is either good or bad depending on the way you look at it. It is an inexorable process and is just neutral, irrespective of its outcome. Change calls for extreme flexibility and alertness of mind. Its objective is generally speaking to bring about improvement so that it can win the widest approval.

A change leader's most important task is selling the idea of change. He trains people to develop a positive approach and acquire skills needed to improve their work environment. The style of functioning varies from person to person. It can be autocratic, participative, supportive or laissez-faire depending upon the group targeted for the change. Its facilitation should be done through stimulating motivation and giving people a chance to make better choices in the light of their understanding and ground realities. It is best to make them fully responsible for their choices as long as they deliver results. The skill of the change leader lies in the ability to get done what he wants done. Resistance is likely to be there as most people avoid doing what they do not want to do. Resistance is a fact of life because all of us including the managers feel comfortable with the way we have been working. Acceptance must begin at the top and resistance to change can be overcome only by first overcoming our own resistance. Resistance to change is best dealt with by accepting it rather than suppressing, avoiding or minimizing it. Change always has an in-built threat, inconvenience or pain in it.

The process of change requires a positive response from all in any organization, without endless negotiations, discussions and debates whether it is necessary or required. There has to be a finality sometime or the other. The change leader has a special responsibility to steer change from the front and not only give advice. Of course the group consensus, wherever possible, should be encouraged, welcomed and implemented. Once the change process has been set in motion, the leader should encourage others to participate actively in it and subtly reduce his role so that others in the group can show their mettle and change their vision.

> Resistance to change is best dealt with by accepting it rather than suppressing, avoiding or minimizing it.

Above all, the change leader should not only change himself but also be equally ardent and convinced about it. The change leader should understand the dynamics, phases and intricacies of a change process. He should also be adept at presenting and selling change as well as dealing adroitly with resistance to change. A change leader should change tactics differently in different circumstances and be ready to take new initiatives and ensure that his strategy leads to minimum disruption and maximum support. One great secret of success in any venture is to either totally eliminate or minimize the feelings of embarrassment and vulnerability of the people with whom one comes in contact in any capacity whether as an elder, a superior or a subordinate.

Simply making resources available is not sufficient. It is strange but true that often people do not ask for help even when it is available and world-class experts can lend a hand. As everywhere those appearing to be in need probably weigh the social cost of appearing to be in need of assistance from others. Nobody wants to admit that he lacks adequate expertise or is incompetent, inferior and the fact that one has to depend on others. It is a kind of upmanship where everybody wants to prove that he is as competent if not more than others who may be experts in their line. Rarely people send out an SOS. They do so only when the heavens are falling. It is for this reason that people conceal their ill-health in important jobs in case they are sacked. I had a boss in an organization who due to severe backache could not even sit up for two hours. Just to hide this fact he had it given it out that he was suffering from viral fever and diarrhoea. After his retirement I asked him as to why he did not tell the truth to the government. He said that either he would have been compulsory retired or sent to an inconsequential job.

It is a different kind of struggle for sticking to power. It is for this reason that the urgent need for assistance is pushed to the background. It is a vicious circle that when you need help you do not to ask for it from your subordinates for fear of appearing to be inadequate in the discharge of your responsibilities. People do not even ask their bosses either for fear of giving a poor impression about themselves. Some people spend their entire career bothering about the impression that their actions will make instead of asking for help. It has to be remembered that everybody cannot be an expert in all spheres of work. Our existence would become easy and our jobs comfortable when we unhesitatingly ask for help

> ★ It is a paradox of human nature that even when help or guidance is needed people do not ask for it for fear of projecting a negative image about themselves.

where it is required for doing our job well. This negative attitude of not asking for help is a great stumbling block to success.

When problems arise some people rarely ask for help even when everything comes to a standstill. On principle nobody wants to seek help from people who are high up in the hierarchy or have more power. It is a paradox of human nature that even when help or guidance is needed people do not ask for it for fear of projecting a negative image about themselves. In peer groups the situation is different as differences between the station in life and position are acceptable or minimum.

As Superintendent of Police of Bidar District in 1966 I received a coded message from the State Police Headquarters giving some top-secret instructions. I worked on it for the whole night but could not decipher it. I realized that it must be something important calling for immediate action. I promptly rang up my neighbouring District Superintendent of Police and asked him to tell me the contents of the message. It was a silly message but all the same, action taken had to reported back within eight hours. He told me what the message contained. I had not rung up the State Criminal Investigation Deputy Inspector General of Police to know what the contents of the message were. It was for the simple reason that I did not want him to know that I had failed even to decipher a simple message. But I had no hesitation in asking a colleague. Similarly, people everywhere are more likely to ask for help from an equal rather than from seniors or superiors. The image building game goes on all the time everywhere. Everybody wants to make sure that he and his position are not threatened or undermined. The answer is to anticipate situations in which people in the organization might need help. Further it should be ensured that they can get it from someone of acceptable or equivalent status. This is possible by having expertise and knowledge anticipated at either downward or upward levels. Almost equal status users and equal status helpers are the best combination.

It is like collecting intelligence where a constable can easily be equated with and can establish rapport with the people in his station of life like petty shopkeepers, taxi and auto drivers, clerks and coolies who would be reluctant to talk even to senior officers. The same is true of use of technology-development plan and acceleration. Turning for help to teammates is a comfortable and appealing proposition. The Government of India has introduced a foundation course of combined training at the time of initial entry for all services including the police, administration, foreign service, customs, income-tax and the other twenty Class I services. This is to build up rapport between the officials of various services who will be progressing in their careers in their respective departments. This has induced a great sense of fellow-feeling and no one has any hesitation in getting in touch with his colleagues whenever any problem arises. Comfortable working makes any system work more coherently. Nobody feels threatened or insecure in asking for assistance and help to keep the administration of the country running.

> ★ It is essential to develop a follow-up programme in order to be successful.

Follow-Up

Dressing is an important part of any person's personality. But there is no dress in the world which will guarantee success. It is your own performance and follow-up which can guarantee success. Follow-up follows actions and carries them forward. It is the effective follow-up which secures success, establishes a reputation of effectiveness and efficiency and develops a sense of responsibility. It is essential to develop a follow-up programme in order to be successful. One left to the memory is only an exercise in futility. This way you can or will do the follow-up only when you remember it. A follow-up requires a lot of effort. Without effort you cannot achieve anything. It is essential to have a system for a follow-up. This way you can strengthen your image. A follow-up requires both time and commitment but it is the only system which will enable you to work efficiently and effectively and enable you to take control of persons, incidents and events. You have to devote some time for a follow-up every day. There has to be an objective of the follow-up which should relate to your work and job. The dividends are heartening. Sometimes the pay-off is instantaneous and sometimes it comes much later. Effective follow-up should be goal-oriented. The progress of follow-up is very often interrupted due to too much paper work, poor memory, too many phone calls, too many interruptions and lack of an established system of follow-up. Sometimes there may be valid and good reasons for such interruptions but they are not valid all the time. It depends on you as to what priority you want or give to a follow-up.

A follow-up is a full time job for some people. Some big companies and almost all state governments have senior officers posted in the national capital for following up their cases, proposals and sanctions with the central government. Once being a liaison officer was considered to be a middleman's or a broker's job but the sheer necessity for expediting work has led to a situation when full time personnel for effective follow-up are necessary. One has to develop an implementation for the job objectives.

Quite often we think that we will manage to finish a particular task in time or send the required report after a day and are unable to do so. This results in tension. One of the best solutions is to write the report immediately and fine-tune it later on. Sometimes there may not be enough time to do so. In that eventuality it will be worthwhile to jot down the major points or decisions taken and complete the report. The best course would be to finish the work there and then. I myself have done the same on my laptop computer. This way you will be able to get it out of the way. Remember that you must always go for the best and not the second best. Give your best performance in any job you might be doing. If you give your best, you have a right to expect the best from others. This way you will build up belief in your ability which will lead to the ultimate realization of your ambition. Always go on expanding your experience by studying and watching methods for better performance. Any goal you set up for yourself should have some plan behind it.

For an effective follow-up you need to have sufficient information about all aspects of the job to be followed up. You can devise any method best suited to you. You could note down the people to be contacted either by telephone, e-mail or a personal gentle reminder. There is no fixed or set method which can help you in achieving results. It will depend upon the situation you find yourself in and the person or company you are dealing with. You should identify the obstacles and barriers which are likely to come in the way of doing an effective follow-up and then remove them. A time comes in the pursuit of a project when interest and enthusiasm wane. It is at this point you should rekindle your faith in yourself and interest in your work and goals by self-induced motivation. Whenever any misgivings or doubts come into your mind about the wisdom of anything you are doing, recall the ultimate benefits you will derive from your success. It is normal and natural even for the most successful to become despondent and abandon projects half-way. But such setbacks should be regarded only as temporary interruptions on the road to success and achievement. You have to deal with your doubts with action, confidence and imagination. For a follow-up you can devise a plan of action regarding jobs, organizations, dates or persons. Never depend upon your memory to remind you as to what is to be done on a particular day. Develop a system for a quick information retrieval system. Have an agenda for the day and follow it up. Devise strategies for a follow-up and stick to it. You should have a strong information base and put it to work for you. You can have a card file according to dates, interests and priorities. On a number of occasions you meet a lot of people and exchange business cards. Instead of just throwing the cards away, write down where you met these people and how they fit in with your business scenario. This system will enable you to remember people who fit in with your scheme of a follow-up. For your scheme to be successful it has to be regular and systematic. You must periodically assess your own

> If you give your best, you have a right to expect the best from others.

operations and whether you need to alter the way you are working. This assessment should also include reinforcing the positive and eliminating the negative. An effective follow-up communicates your competence. For a proper impact it is equally important to redeem the promises made. You should maintain a report card of your achievements. Even self-employed persons should have a progress report on themselves so that they are aware of their achievements or failures. It will help them to compare with what they are doing and what they have done previously. A progress report on yourself will help you track down as to where you are spending time and whether there are any aberrations in your functioning effectively. You should do your best at all times. It is not necessary nor is it always possible that you succeed in everything you do. You can only do your best and nothing more than that. Life is a roller-coaster. There are very few things you can control. But if you control your life's graph with a positive approach and confidence you will

> ★ You should have a strong information base and put it to work for you.

always achieve what you have set out to achieve. Remember that the journey is as important as the goal. Enjoy your life both during the journey as well as after you have reached your destination. Negative and irrational thinking has never helped anybody. Be assured it will not help you.

How To Win Over Enemies And Antagonists

Creating, sustaining and nurturing negativity is a matter of great personal loss to the person who is doing it whether consciously or unconsciously. A brilliant boss or a leader who does not take counsel ruins his own chances of success. As the very future and sometimes very existence in an organization may depend upon the goodwill of the boss, many employees will be rarely willing to point out that the boss is either suggesting or pursuing a disastrous course. If you are feeling inspired, show it and let your actions reflect it. Keep on upgrading your skills. It does not pay to enhance hostility. Do not always try to control or influence the decisions of people under and around you. Get into the habit of seeking inputs from others. You may be better informed than them but always playing the role of implacable big brother intimidates the expression of initiative from others. It would be foolish to take credit for the work of people who are the backbone of the organization.

Never use work hours, pay benefits, overtime assignment, compensation and incentives, dress codes, office facilities, job requirements, working conditions to destabilize or intimidate good workers.

Every day gives the people in authority an opportunity to make their presence and power felt in an aggressive or a negative way. This can harm both the organization and the individuals. It will lead to dissatisfaction and resentment. Negativity grows in geometric progression to the negative role played by the boss.

Transparency and consistency in any organization are the solutions for the bad effects of manager's whims and idiosyncrasies. It is true that everyone cannot be the same. God has not made two individuals alike. Everybody cannot be treated in the same way. The boss has the right to reward merit according to well-defined standards of evaluation. Everybody has a right to a fair and an equal treatment. Aggression should not be used to subdue people. Let people know that it is their work and not their need to please you which will get them appreciation, advancement or other rewards. This level of transparency is a must for any organization which wants to grow and expand.

Communication is a major problem in any organization. There is never enough of it. Give people a chance to express their ideas. Let people know what is expected of them. Never keep employees in the dark and take all possible help when a crisis comes along. Clarity of objectives motivates and enables people to perform better. Do not interfere if they are working well. Basic to every organization is communication as every organization depends on people, their attitudes, attention, understanding and motivation. These factors are critical.

Organizations and their workers want growth. However, growth is possible only by training and change in the aptitude as well as the attitude of the people who work in any organization. Ambitious employees are eager for training. The organization should arrange to give it to them in plenty. Training the trainable is an important fact. This can conserve resources as well as enhance the value and utility of the trained to the organization. It is the duty of the boss to look after his workers and others in the organization. Grooming people thoroughly in understanding and working towards the fulfilment of the vision, values and goals of your organization is a pre-requisite to productivity. Negativity at every hour and every minute should be reduced. There is no such thing as a 'positive negativity'.

Different situations with different objectives and different problems call for a unique and effective presentation. This is the only way in which you can send any message straight to the heart of the people in the organization. It is a

Let people know what is expected of them.

challenge to be faced imaginatively every day. Each presentation should be tailored to suit the demands of a particular situation and a particular group of people or audience. Strategies which will help in effectively dealing with any problem are given below.

Always Be Conscious Of The Value Of Time

The ideal limit for presenting a case study or a talk is 30 minutes. Audience concentration is very high either in the beginning or towards the fag-end of a presentation. This factor should be kept in mind while talking to a group or when giving a presentation. There is nothing worse than a presenter who says that he is about to finish and continues talking for another half an hour. Close all your presentations effectively. The last impression is the one that lasts. Tell the audience: " It will be useful to keep these five points in mind" and re-emphasize the points. Repeat your points, if necessary, but in a pleasant way. You can also use dramatic contrasts to reinforce a point. For example: "Ten years ago we were a small organization. Today we are one of the biggest in our field in the whole country." You can also present your ideas as questions rather than direct statements. This challenges the audience and creates a feeling of anticipation. This strategy also facilitates a dialogue with the audience. It is better to have a dialogue rather than a monologue.

Simplification promotes clarity of expression and facilitates comprehension. It also points towards focusing. Emphasize your point by stringing together several small chunks of information to build up a simple conclusion. Make the last sentence a simple summary of the situation cleverly delivered after a short pause. Another alternative technique is to carefully build up a series of points opposing your main argument and then knock them all down with a single argument. In this competitive world it is the effort of each organization to remain ahead of its competitors. The effort normally is to generate more profits, possess a respectable corporate image and still remain in tune with the times. Both the survival and the progress of an organization depends on the individuals who continuously look for new ways to add value to the company. Having the right people for the right job plays an important role in determining an organization's path towards success. Organizations have to be innovative for getting the best people. Only those people who are willing to act as self-starters and have the right attitude towards life and the vision, mission and values of the organization can take it forward. Such people strengthen the corporate values and culture. Achievements and not vague promises distinguish them from others. Do not give the impression that you are not a willing worker. Managers controlled their subordinates in the past but now the policy of encouraging them and making winners out of them is paying huge dividends. Individuals want to work in a free environment. It has been demonstrated that when employees are given responsibility, their efficiency and effectiveness increase automatically.

Organizations in today's competitive world now look for talent and the cutting edge of expertise for their growth.

Specialization is 'in' now. Expertise and the ability to deliver are the only factors which increase competitive advantages. Knowledge and the will to adapt are positive assets. The contribution made towards the success of the organization as well as developing unique skills and core competencies are what matter both for short-term and long-term issues.

> ★ Having the right people for the right job plays an important role in determining an organization's path towards success.

The following 'Do's' will help managers in every organization.

1. Every manager should hone skills in his specialization and core competence in some field. It should be demonstrated in the organization that a manager is a manager by virtue of competence and not because of seniority or recommendations.

2. They should make it a point to communicate to their bosses what they have contributed to the organization.

3. They should make sure that they are fully aware of the global trends or the position of their competitors in the same field.

4. They should always try to upgrade their skills and make sure that their skills are fully utilized. Competence and experience are the best testimonials. It is the duty of the managers to make sure that the skills and competencies imparted by them in the organization are used to the optimum.

Delegation Leads To More Output

Delegation is a tricky business. The idea of delegation should not be to simply 'dump' distasteful, boring or uninteresting work on someone else. The objective should be to make sure that a job which need not be done by you, gets done quickly and successfully. Delegation is more difficult and sensitive, particularly, when it is lateral like asking a colleague, a family member or a friend to stand in for you and help you out. However, a kind of understanding or even a formalized agreement about the projects, goals and objectives and how they should be achieved will lessen stress. It will be clear to all as to which part of the job will be done by whom.

Strengths And Weaknesses

When delegating a job to someone else it is important to keep in mind the person's competence, talents, achievements in the area of specialization and his existing workload. The secret of successful delegation is to delegate to someone who can successfully complete the work assigned. Delegating a job to someone who does not have the time, skills, resources, experience, enthusiasm or willingness is as good as ensuring the failure of the project of delegation and frustration for the delegator and the delegatee. It is equally important to delegate jobs to persons related to their skill and competence level. Assignment of the work should not be substantially below the skill level of the delegatee.

A project can be delegated to the most junior person who in the perception of the delegator is capable of successfully

completing the work. It will build up his
morale. It will give him confidence besides
saving the organization time and expense
of engaging a highly paid person for the
same work. Moreover, it will save the time
of the senior executives to concentrate
on other quality work.

> Never delegate a job without setting completion deadlines.

Delegation should be a mixed bag containing both innovative and interesting projects along with work which might be considered a drudgery. It will wear out the enthusiasm of the team members if you only give them routine work. Delegation should also provide an opportunity to help others grow and expand their skills and increase competence. It is also a way for the delegator to get routine chores done. The delegator can challenge the delegatee to do more difficult assignments in the future. This will satisfy his ego and the delegator need not worry that he will be overburdened. It is best to keep a delegation log so that the delegator does not forget as to what work, when and to whom it was delegated and when it was expected to be completed. Along with the delegation, keeping track of what projects you gave to whom and the date of their completion is equally important. We all tend to forget things and so it is best to write them down. Never delegate a job without setting completion deadlines. Give your delegatee a firm deadline along with the assigned job. However, it must be clearly understood that the delegatee does not take the ultimate responsibility for completion of the job. Never be a nagger wasting all your time asking, "When will the job be done?"

Break The Job Into Chunks

Since the ultimate responsibility for completing a delegated assignment or a project lies with the delegator it is not the best policy to wait until two days before the deadline to see what kind of progress the delegatee is making. It is best to set milestones or sub-deadlines for completing a project, section by section or part by part. Any job broken up into smaller pieces is much easier for the delegatee to handle and complete. It is desirable to set up a series of natural follow-up points throughout the project. Instead of checking up on the last day of the deadline, check up with the delegatee at each sub-deadline for the progress of the job.

Do not indulge in a guessing game as to how far a delegatee has completed a project at any point. Ask the delegatee about his progress at regular intervals. Establish milestones for reviewing his progress. It is a perfect reason and justification for a meeting or a written report. This enables the delegator to discuss any problem the delegatee might have run into, any additional resources he might need and make any adjustments to the schedule for completing the job. In this way you will not be surprised at any changes in the way of doing things or changes in the completion schedule. People doing a particular task should know in advance the end result expected from them for the delegated job. That might appear obvious. But it is generally seen that few people do it thoroughly enough. The result is a garbled output. Furnish the delegated persons with

> Delegation is about letting go of a job you feel that somebody can do it for you equally competently.

enough inputs and help so that they do not keep coming back far more frequently than what is reasonable. The entire purpose of delegation is to save the precious time of the delegator for doing more important jobs. The very purpose of delegation is lost if the delegatee has to keep on clarifying some

> ★ It is desirable to set up a series of natural follow-up points throughout the project.

point or the other either on the phone or in meetings regarding the progress of the work. If this is happening frequently, then it is time to review clearly whether something has been properly delegated or the person concerned to whom the task has been delegated finds himself unequal to the task or does not have the qualifications or competence to do it. If necessary, review thoroughly and take a decision to reassign it to some more competent person. However, once you are convinced that the delegatee has a firm grasp and can deliver the expected end result give him enough freedom to decide how to accomplish the assigned job. Delegation should not be confused with 'micro-managing'. Delegation is about letting go of a job you feel that somebody can do it for you equally competently. The boss or delegatee should only be concerned in the first place with the end results without bothering or caring as to how it is or was accomplished. Give a pat on the back to the delegatee and give credit where credit is due! No one likes to work hard on a job for someone else and not receive at least some appreciation and may be some glory. In this way you can encourage the delegatees to work harder for you in the long run. What a delegatee needs is a bit of praise, appreciation and some credit and if you give it he will feel more than compensated for the labour he has put in to accomplish a project.

Outsourcing Can Buy You Time

Outsourcing is one way to get the help of outside professionals or services to take on part of the workload whether in the government or private sector. It helps a person who may not have the time or the expertise or there may be periodic busy periods or one needs to do more and in time etc. The following are the ways by which you can increase your productivity and save time and money. Train people to perform. If you do not have the time to train people working with you, delegate this job by outsourcing employees. This will give you more time for performing your work better. Getting the work done from outside will save you on technology costs as you will not have to spend money on buying new equipment or learning new software to complete some jobs. This will allow you to spend more time on the things which matter to you and your organization. You will also be saved the hassle of interviewing candidates and giving them regular jobs whether you have work or not for them. Outsourcing will consequently mean less paper work for your organization so you need not bother about the employees tax forms, medical leave, holidays, workers' compensation, scheduling holidays and retirement plans etc. This will give you more time for concentrating on your work. This policy of outsourcing will also save you money on hiring or buying extra office or work space to complete certain jobs. You can then use the money you save on more productive channels or for meeting the needs which can push you up professionally. You can also work faster by outsourcing as well as getting the name of a good worker who has the skill and competence to deliver whatever he or she promises.

Delegate For Success

Delegation is a powerful tool which can be used everywhere. If there is a proper delegation in the workplace it will lead to an increase in productivity, advancement, prosperity as well as in preparing juniors for taking on higher responsibilities. At home, delegation can lead to the learning and sharing of responsibilities and teamwork by the family members as well as learning the importance of family values. Reluctance to delegate is due to the desire for perfectionism as well as lack

> ★ Getting the work done from outside will save you on technology costs as you will not have to spend money on buying new equipment or learning new software to complete some jobs.

of understanding of the importance of delegation. Delegation can and should be mastered and this can be done over a period of time. It requires patience but the payoff is much bigger. If we desire to accomplish more, make better use of our time, find time for more important projects, work or for leisure activities it is important to learn to delegate. Delegating invariably involves making use of the experience and expertise of competent persons. Without assigning the job to the right person the delegation will be a flop. The right person can be in terms of qualifications or a person who has a stake in the success of the project or the job or a person who is enthusiastic and dedicated by habit and nature. It is important to provide necessary assistance to the delegatee and clearly explain to him his responsibilities. However, the final accountability of the job lies with the delegator.

It Does Not Have To Be Perfect

Perfectionism can be dangerous in some ways in the process of delegation. Progress and perfection go together to some extent. Absolute perfection is an illusion because the more you accomplish the more you feel is left to achieve. What is important is the completion of certain tasks rather than doing them in a particular way. It is important to remember that there can be more than one way of completing a task. Do not insist on getting a job done exactly as you would have done it. Your way of doing things may be a good way. But do not commit the mistake of saying that it is the only way to do something. What is important is to get a job done properly but not necessarily your way. Frequently, the delegatees come up with new innovative or even quicker, easier ways to reach the same result. It is important not to discourage initiative as it will discourage the delegatee to be enthusiastic, creative and result-oriented. Do not let the quest for perfectionism hinder the delegation process.

Stay In Touch

★ Do not insist on getting a job done exactly as you would have done it.

A follow-up is crucial to the success of a project. It not only encourages learning and provides the delegatee with much-needed support but also ensures accountability. When you are reviewing regularly the chances of something missing or being bungled are greatly reduced. Regular scheduled observations or meetings will ensure the timely and acceptable completion of your project.

Give Credit Where Credit Is Due

The positive end result of successful delegation is that the project is completed and all parties are satisfied. Self-satisfaction and an inner pride over a well-done job are the ultimate rewards. The material remuneration is also equally important. If bonuses and gifts are not possible then verbal kudos are just as encouraging and substantial. Recognition can be in the form of an acknowledgement in the organization's newsletter, a printed certificate or the award of special privileges. Recognition and appreciation are essential to ensure a willing and pleasant working relationship in the future. Delegation may sometimes be difficult. Never give an impression of being overworked or a beast of burden. The very idea of being overworked is stressful and non-productive, so be a willing worker or manager and aim at delegation for success.

Delegation Dilemma

It is a well-known fact that we all have 24 hours in each day, 7 days a week. If you multiply that gives a total of 168 hours a week. But the full 168 hours are not available to us as we have to subtract time for sleeping, eating and other activities. Let us assume that on an average 8 hours rest per day is required. Sleep is something that cannot be postponed indefinitely. You have to catch up on it sooner or later. It takes one third of the week, that is to say, 8 hours for all 7 nights of the week. Some may still need more sleep whereas some others could do with less. Another 4 hours are needed on an average for eating, dressing, travelling, telephoning, watching television, reading newspapers, meeting visitors, chatting with family members. Thus, if we subtract a total of 84 hours out of 168 hours we are left with 84 hours for all we wish to do which includes our professional jobs, entertaining ourselves, socialization, reading newspapers, answering phone calls, improving our skills or commuting. Assuming that you spend all the time working when you are not sleeping you will have only 112 hours per week to complete all your projects. In actual practice though it is totally unpractical and unrealistic to expect it. If you decide to do everything yourself you will be limiting your potential to a ceiling of 84 to 112 hours. But if you can get others to do a few things for you, you will be able to increase your output as well as results.

This is the underlying idea behind the concept of delegation. Delegation, plainly speaking, is using or buying someone else's time when either you do not have the time or the expertise to do something but you need to get it done in your own or the best interests of your organization. Truly speaking, all of us are delegating all the time both consciously and unconsciously. Any of us could go to the post office, rent our own postal box and then each day take a trip to the post office to retrieve our mail. Most people, however, make the sensible decision that it is best to have the letters delivered to us to save our time and money. Once I took my family for dinner to a restaurant. Conservatively, both directly and indirectly, more than 150 people were involved in the production of that meal and for giving us a decent dinner. The farmer grew the vegetables first by cultivating the land or getting it cultivated. He bought the fertilizers which were produced in a factory employing hundreds of people. The factory ran on electricity which was produced in a hydroelectric project employing thousands of people. The factory itself was fabricated in another factory employing thousands of people. The farmer used the tractor which was again manufactured in another factory. The produce of vegetables, rice and meat was transported to the market which gave jobs to the transporters which enabled them to earn their livelihood. It was further bought by the restaurant which cooked and converted the raw material into the meal for which I paid a few hundreds. Probably hundreds, if not thousands, worked for producing that meal. Someone planted the wheat to make the bread, someone had to pick the tomatoes to make the ketchup and someone had drilled the oil out of the ground to power the delivery truck to your restaurant. It is a perfect example of delegation. Imagine if this delegation and interdependence had not existed each one of us would have to grow his or her own vegetables. Household chores exist on delegation. Many people have earned their livelihood from one meal.

> Delegation is a concept of satisfaction of an individual's personal needs.

The History Of Delegation

Earlier there was no concept of delegation. If present, it was hardly practised. In primitive societies if you wanted to eat or wear something you had to produce it. The concepts of restaurants or inns or hotels are of comparatively recent origin.

If you wanted to eat non-vegetarian food you had to hunt for it. Similarly, for housing, an individual had to go into the woods, clear the land, cut the wood, make it into logs and build his own house. There were no contractors or real estate agents or builders. Delegation is a concept of satisfaction of an individual's personal needs. This has been possible as a result of the agricultural and industrial revolutions which have enabled mass production of inexpensive goods and services for the market. This has led to the payment of relatively higher wages to workers enabling them to buy such products. If you and I had to do everything ourselves, create our own food, clothing, housing, transportation, education etc. we would probably lose 90% of what we have now or have an achievement level of only 10%.

To Delegate Or Not To Delegate

We are all delegating all the time, sometimes even without realizing that we are doing so. For instance, when we are travelling in a chauffeur-driven car we have delegated the responsibility of driving to the driver so the question is not whether we delegate or not. The real question to ask is how much and how far to delegate. The delegation can open the door to greater and greater success as we have a ceiling of 112 hours available to each one of us every week assuming that we work for 16 hours all seven days. Depending upon the type of work delegated we can add another 50 to 100 productive hours per week. The hardest

★
Delegation is not 'micro-managing' and always looking over the shoulders of the delegatee.

part of delegation is finding out the right people to delegate and then plan for them. It is also developing an attitude of trusting people and their judgement that they can and will do things as well as we can. Delegation is the opposite of the concept that: "If you want a job well done you must do it yourself." You should have a look at all the tasks to be done during the day and the following day and then decide whether doing it yourself is the best use of your time. If it is not, then figure out ways to delegate them. If it is something that only you can or should do, then personally tackle it.

By applying the principle of delegation you can make your days and output more productive. The whole point behind the drill of delegation is to save you time so that you can do more productive work. Once you delegate and feel that the delegatee has a firm grasp and will produce the expected end result allow him enough freedom to decide about the methods of accomplishing the tasks. Delegation is not 'micro-managing' and always looking over the shoulders of the delegatee. It is about letting go of a job you did not do or did not want to do in the first place. As long as a job gets done and the necessary results are achieved nobody will care as to how it was accomplished or who did it. The important thing is the final outcome.

Look At Costs Versus Benefits

Occasionally, all of us spend a lot of time on very low priority work like addressing 150 envelopes for a routine greeting on a festive occasion, cleaning the house or cutting dried plants in the garden. It is not something that is going to tremendously improve your quality of life despite its being a time-consuming activity. The rewards for doing this kind of job is not in direct proportion to the investment of time and energy. These kind of jobs break the monotony only once in a while and at the best are diversionary. Their completion does not make a major impact or improve the quality of our lives but some such jobs have to be done to keep up the contacts and as a part of the service or means of livelihood. If not done they can erode away home, career, health, peace of mind and cause serious problems in life.

These routine chores are the perfect candidates for your 'Not-to-do' list. They are the items of work that should really be done but they need not necessarily be done by you at the cost of high value time. The work that could be delegated could be house maintenance, cleaning, washing and ironing clothes, grocery shopping, preparation of meals, paperwork-filing, mailing, organizing, follow-up with letters, e-mails and routine typing, running errands, visits to banks and post offices, gardening, car service and maintenance, travel, meetings and event arrangements.

The above is only a suggested list and not a totally exhaustive one. If you enjoy doing even a few routine things, then do them. I like, for example, gardening or browsing through some sites on the Internet. Even if a task is time-consuming but fills you with renewed energy, a sense of satisfaction and creativity, the payoff is worth it regardless of the cost benefit ratio. Activities vary from person to person. Some may prefer gardening while others may like kite flying. One person

★ It is for each one of us to decide as to what is high priority work in our own scheme of things.

may like to do something himself whereas another one may like to get the same work done by others. It is all a question of what energizes and cheers you, fills your life with joy and what you look forward to doing. If any activity fits this description, then do it yourself. Put other less pleasurable chores on your 'Not-to-do' list. The acid test of all this exercise is to determine whether this is the best possible use of your time. When writing the 'Not-to-do' list which is the opposite of the 'Do' list, do not get overwhelmed by daily chores like paying bills, house cleaning and writing reports. This may result in paying too little attention to our real priorities which may get neglected in the process. It is for each one of us to decide as to what is high priority work in our own scheme of things. These priorities can range from looking after the family and spending time with it or concentrating on achieving results in the job in which we are engaged in. Only you yourself have to decide as to where you will get the biggest returns of your investments of time and money.

Finding An Alternative

After you have made a list of items to be delegated then decide who should be asked to do the work to be done. Should your family, subordinates, a co-worker or other colleagues be of some assistance? If you have people working for you like administrative clerks, assistants, typists or stenographers, make full use of them. Hire a freelancer to help with household and business tasks that you do not have time for but are essential to your success. Remember that if you are taking the help of your colleagues and co-workers you have to be ready to help them when they ask for it. Remember also that asking for help is not a one-sided affair and you are not the only one who asks for help. It is a two-way street. Nevertheless, you have to decide what you want to delegate. Then go whole hog and, if required, be willing to ask for help.

Do Not Wait For Tomorrow

Innovation is a crucial requirement in the ever-changing milieu in the modern world. It requires constant learning and systematic updating. To be effective it needs to be built into the work culture. Innovation needs perseverance, intelligence and an ability to give shape to bold ideas for further development on a continuous basis. It is important to constantly ask a question whether the existing practices, procedures and precedents encourage or discourage innovations. Assess your weaknesses and strengths. This is the only way to develop a new work culture which is willing to try out new innovations. Unless new ideas are translated into action they are as good as non-existent. Plans and proposals have to be turned into reality. The entire workplace has to be turned into an innovation machine.

Examples of bad management and bad bosses teach us how not to be like them. Bad managers can teach you more than any management school of the pitfalls of thinking. They will help you understand that unpleasant or humiliating events of life are the soil in which success can grow. I wanted to go to Bangalore in 1965 to purchase a car which had been allotted to me by the Government. As I was the District Police Chief, Bidar District summons to the State Capital by the State Police Chief were enough for my official visit. But my immediate boss, the then DIG Belgaum, came to know that I was going to combine my official visit with private work. He was one of those officers who would go out of the way to deny others anything which he felt could be useful to people working with him, so he made sure that I could not go. During my initial service I also had a boss, my Superintendent of Police who never took interest in my training. Similarly, in the Ministry of Commerce where I was a Director, a clean-shaven Sikh who was the Head of the Ministry would throw his weight around during my tenure when I was Superintendent of Police. I had a Director of CBI who never smiled at anybody. He also suspected that well-dressed people were corrupt and dishonest. These bad examples taught me not to be petty-minded or a tyrannical boss when it was my turn to be the Chief.

> Unless new ideas are translated into action they are as good as non-existent.

Big achievements and positive results emerge from right decisions which in turn are based on right inputs. Selection of necessary information and facts can only lead to informed decisions. Faulty decisions can destroy both careers and business enterprises. Facts are an important ingredient. But do not waste your time in collecting and analyzing data leaving hardly any time for actual work. Too much analysis is sometimes counter-productive. A fixed time schedule and a fixed deadline is the ideal solution for dealing with most problems. Some mistakes are inevitable in life. The important thing is to profit from them and move back on to the track of success. Sometimes the very act of collecting of facts is used as an excuse to postpone decisions. This is true of the government where important decisions are postponed in the name of collection of facts, inter-departmental advice and interminable meetings. I was both a witness and a mute party to such an exercise in the ministry of commerce which was responsible for implementing a little known legislation called The Enemy Property Act. Under the Act an officer of the level of Deputy Secretary to the Government of India was working as Custodian of Enemy Property. This post was created in 1939 during the Second World War to seize and manage the properties of enemy nationals belonging to the countries at war with British India. Pakistan whose nationals' properties are even now being managed by the Government of India has found a solution to the problem but we continue to adhere to laws which hardly serve the interests of India or the Indians. This is one case of an atrocious example of the government not moving with the times.

★ Too much analysis is sometimes counter-productive.

In life the more you do there is still something left to be done. There is a tremendous pressure to make more money, to discharge more duties, to have more fun, to make more contacts in life, to rise higher in your job and have a set of accomplishments to your credit. The result is that in this rat race it is our relationship with ourselves and our perception of ourselves which takes a beating. Circumstances compel people to be competitive and accomplish more and more leading to stress. Despite all the luxuries, comforts and money, happiness is something which is not available for a price in the market. Despite all these contradictions a person's social standing remains pegged to his monetary value. The present culture is not to have things but to have many things whether it is the number of telephones, cars, air conditioners or computers in the house. It is immaterial whether one can use only one telephone or one air conditioner at a time.

The world by tradition and practice is unkind to failure. It also disregards all those who have outlived their utility either healthwise or agewise. Any failure is cause enough to upset equations by those who might have once lionized you. Success has an aura about it.

> Leadership is not fire-fighting and solving problems on an ad hoc basis.

Success attracts success. Ultimately the twilight of career and life arrives for everybody. One's reputation, prominence in life and centrestage position depends only on hits.

An organization which wishes to have a better and a different future must be prepared for innovations. Results do not lie with the organization but with those who interact with it or use its services. Force can yield the desired results. It is the free will exercised by individuals which contributes towards success. Leadership comes by earmarking sufficient resources and whatever else is required to seize and cash in on opportunities. Leadership is not fire-fighting and solving problems on an ad hoc basis. Leadership emerges out of selecting and using the best options for forging ahead with the available resources. All management is directed towards producing and getting results. Success comes from updating skills and knowledge. The management should make it clear to the people working in the organization to identify and update the specialization they require to translate the corporate or business objectives into a reality.

It Is Survival Of The Fittest All The Way

There are plenty of suggestions and methods which can bring about change and require new initiatives. Any change is bound to cause tension and resentments when new economic and social values replace the old order and society. Bringing about a change for the progress and development of any organization is a very important managerial responsibility. A lot of research material is available suggesting appropriate strategies to develop the best management approach. Approaches in bringing about change are bound to be different in different organizations because they exist in different environments. The management style of one company is not strictly relevant to the others though the good points can be picked up from each. There is bound to be some failure in initiatives to bring about change. In some it can be as high as 60%. The only way to bring about improvement is to be on the look out for new initiatives for the change. As long as this approach continues there is hope that mankind will move towards new horizons. Most management gurus have similar experiences, approaches and suggestions so they offer almost similar advice. The fact, however, remains that it is best to treat any activity or any organization just like a human being. The change should be brought about in acceptable and retainable doses by the people working in it without losing sight of the main objective and desirable outcomes. Nobody is infallible and despite best efforts the outcome cannot be predicted. Factors responsible for the disturbance of equilibrium including those caused by change can lead to

> Mass belief in a particular course of action can lead to spectacular results.

unpredictable situations. However, the bottomline is that only by bringing about change can you bring about a desired result. As the old saying goes: "Nothing ventured, nothing gained", is not a cliché but a reality. The involvement of the maximum number of people who are led by decisive leaders can only lead to success. It is always the few who decide for the majority. The method of integrating the managers and employees can be done through working conferences, lectures, and question and answer sessions. This will help in overhauling the vision, relationship and philosophy along with the organizational patterns ideally suited to deal with the new realities. It is best to carry people along and not allow them to simmer. Mass belief in a particular course of action can lead to spectacular results. No pocket of resistance, however small or ostensibly insignificant, should be ignored. Because of the very nature of human existence and unpredictable behaviour patterns it is not possible to give a model which will hold good for all times to come. Situations, environments and persons vary from place to place. The only reality is that change is both inescapable and inevitable. Most persons are uncomfortable with change and are unwilling to take chances. However, solid performers are willing to take a chance and try to find better ways of greater and greater achievement. Those who believe in the status quo will resist all change like most government servants. Perhaps the organizations would be better off without them. The best way to deal with these various groups is to convert them to your viewpoint. This will help people

> It is best not to shoot the dissenters but to understand their point of view as there may be some substance in what they say.

understand the situation as well as help and guide the employees who sincerely want to help the organization improve, grow and prosper. It is best not to shoot the dissenters but to understand their point of view as there may be some substance in what they say. Discussing with those who refuse to join the bandwagon will leave any organization with 'Yes men' only who are not the best agents of change but only time-servers. The trouble with all advice, notwithstanding its utility, is that it is mostly piecemeal. Strategies, structures and systems are just the hardware of the organization. Change is possible if it flows from top to bottom to yield quick results. If it is a commercial organization then the financial targets will dominate all its activities and will be on top of the agenda. Financial incentives are regularly used as the motivators of change to align people working anywhere with the interests of private management as well as in the government. All management consultancies hired for crores of rupees are meant to motivate and inform employees so that they can perform better. Building a sustainable competitive advantage and competencies is the best means for safeguarding both short-term and long-term interests of any organization. Maintaining high standards requires an environment in which employees are motivated and emotionally committed to accepting new challenges for achieving continuing excellence and solving new problems that continually arise in the ongoing process towards success. It is the tireless efforts put in by the team of professionals which

> A powerful vision enables you to tap your inner strengths, resources and potentials that you did not even know existed in you.

contribute to success. Success is both challenging and gruelling. The ultimate result of succeeding will always be immensely satisfying and gratifying. One always acquires experience and learns lessons along the way. What is essential for success is to have a broad vision and the capacity to think big. It is the vision which leads you and your team towards that which at the first instance seems unachievable. It is important to keep the collective imagination and passion of

> As a leader your actions should be able to stand the test of integrity and public or organizational scrutiny.

the team fired with a fervent desire to succeed with a single-minded dedication. A powerful vision enables you to tap your inner strengths, resources and potentials that you did not even know existed in you. Success has a built-in failure element but the courage to take risks is equally important. If one always thought of plane crashes, one would not stir out of one's house. Planes are the safest when not flying and on the ground but they have not been invented to stay at the airport. However, strategies of intensive training and flying by pilots have made the air journey not only risk-free but also the fastest mode of transport. No vision which aims at magnificent plans can be safe. A reputation is always built on values and a capacity to deliver. The basic fundamental values, no matter what the situation might be, should be practised as something totally non-negotiable. This will make your success worthwhile. Demonstrate transparency in your working as well as in your core values. As a leader your actions should be able to stand the test of integrity and public or organizational scrutiny. This behaviour and conduct will build tremendous self-confidence which is most needed when any organization is heading

> ★ Winning is reaching the depth of your own potential and utilizing it to its fullest.

downwards. Take whatever course seems best to you. Go ahead and do what you believe should be done. Ignore any prophets of gloom and pessimists who may come cross your path. Self-confidence is absolutely fundamental to success. If you do not have confidence in yourself there is no way your employees or people you are dealing with will have in you.

Select the best of workers, intellectuals, managers for your organization. In short, enlist the services of the best people. Organizations and the best of plans accomplish nothing without the best men to conceive and implement plans. Organizations succeed or fail because of the people working for them and in them. Have a knack of selecting people who have the capacity to anticipate and see around corners which others have failed to notice. Other elements like loyalty, integrity, a high-energy drive, emotional maturity and an overpowering desire to get things done are, other assets which should be developed and encouraged in the employees. There should be literally an obsessive commitment to give the highest quality of services in whatever sphere you or your organization are engaged in. Everybody wants the best quality at the cheapest rates all over the world. The demand for high quality services and goods is the direct result of globalization. Quality is the first pre-requisite both for survival and success these days. Always aim to win and be the best man in your kind of job. Rendering shoddy service is something that will have no takers anywhere in the world.

Never compromise on the quality of goods and services.

Winning should be your constant motto. Never feel guilty or apologetic about success. All the struggle in life is about winning and succeeding. Of course the effort stretches you and the people working for you. It is a decent way to give yourself a purpose and a new sense of direction and energy. Playing should be fair and above board. Never cut corners or take short cuts to success which call for sustained efforts. A success achieved through short cuts will be short-lived. It will not give you the satisfaction of winning. Winning is reaching the depth of your own potential and utilizing it to its fullest. You should be your own competitor. Believe in your God. He will help you in your difficulties. It is worthwhile to mention a story as to how God helps all of us in our difficulties. "One night a man had a dream. He dreamt that he was walking along the beach with the Lord. Then scenes from his life flashed across the sky. In each scene he saw two sets of footprints in the sand, one belonging to him and the other to the Lord. When the last scene flashed before him he looked back at the footprints in the sand. He found that many times along the path of his life there was only one set of footprints He also noted that it happened at the most difficult and the saddest times in his life. This really disturbed him and he questioned the Lord thus: 'Lord you said that once I decided to follow You, You would walk with me all the way. But I have noticed that during the most troublesome times in my life there is only one set of footprints. I don't understand why when I needed You the most You would leave me.' The Lord smiled and gently replied, 'My precious, precious child, I love you and I would

> Organizations succeed or fail because of the people working for them and in them.

never leave you. During your times of trial and suffering when you see only one set of footprints I carried you in my arms.'"

> The first important step towards your happiness will mean examining your fears and coming up with workable solutions.

We know quite often what should be done. The hesitation arises while taking the first step. It could be that one is feeling too scared to make a selection out of the choices available. The real reason is that you may be apprehensive that you may make the wrong choice. It could also be that you are afraid to make a positive change in your life because you may have to make a departure from all that is familiar and comfortable. Most people do not want a change even though they may be unhappy with their present lot. In case your present lifestyle is not paying you the dividends which are rightfully yours, you should challenge the boundaries of your existence and strive for greater happiness and satisfaction. The first important step towards your happiness will mean examining your fears and coming up with workable solutions. It is important to examine your fear of making the required change? What is the worst that can happen if you go ahead with your plans? Do you fear failure or success? For example, if you want to improve your competence and qualifications for a better job and want to study further then ask yourself as to why you are dragging your feet in doing something about upgrading your skills? Are you afraid that you will not do well and a make a fool of yourself in the eyes of your friends and colleagues? Are you afraid that you will have to leave your present location and move away from your family and present friends? Are you afraid that despite your higher qualifications you may still not get the job of your choice? The solution is to deal with your fears one at a time. If you are afraid of not doing well in the higher course of study put in your best efforts and work hard. If you are apprehensive of moving away from your friends and family, explain to yourself that this kind of fear is normal. Focus instead on to how you can stay in touch with old friends and at the same time make new friends.

Finally, if you are doubtful whether a higher qualification will change your career for the better, do some serious soul searching to determine how you can make the best use of your competence and qualifications. Look for opportunities to improve your life instead of constantly complaining that

> Small steps and small risks enable us to face the big difficulties in phases over a period of time.

everything is wrong in your life. In life, many times, a few situations arise where courage is the only thing which can stand you in good stead. Do not try to tackle every problem at once. Challenge one problem or one apprehension at a time. This is the only way you will not feel overwhelmed and build up your confidence as well. Take small steps one at a time. Small steps and small risks enable us to face the big difficulties in phases over a period of time. Separate your apprehensions and fears from reality. Instead of constantly worrying that things will go wrong, believe that everything will turn out to be the best. Make a second nature of being positive in your life and your work.

Be constantly conscious of your attitude so that you can adjust and do midcourse correction when it starts becoming negative. Pat yourself on the back for your achievements and your 'winner' attitude. Keep focused on the positive in your work, life and relationships. Go on reinforcing and encouraging yourself with positive thoughts. Stick to your goals. It is very important to avoid negative people who radiate negative impulses and vibrations. It is best to associate with positive people. Do not let the negativity of others influence you, trouble you and depress you. The world is full of such people. Never let others dictate what you should do with and in your life. Do not let someone's bad mood rub off on you. Protecting your attitude is important to your success and happiness. Visualize yourself succeeding especially in areas where you are fearful to enter. Visualization is a powerful technique. It can make heroes out of zeros. Visualize yourself as a successful professional, a successful writer or a successful speaker. Visualize the appreciation and applause on your success. Always stick with your goal even when things seem impossible to endure or get tough. Above all be patient with yourself. Keep on constantly recharging your courage and determination. Always keep calm. Practice deep breathing and other relaxation exercises before tackling any difficult task. It will enable you to take on any tough job with a positive and a winning approach.

5

COMMUNICATING
FOR RESULTS

The skills of listening and writing are used the least. Listening is least taught but done most. A lot of time is spent in listening to your boss, your colleagues and your staff everyday. If we are not getting the most out of listening then it is time to hone this skill. Look for any quality or skill you can use. Listen to what is really being said and make notes if you need to. Focus on the content and not on the person who is speaking. Do not let your feelings or prejudices either for or against the speaker affect your faculties to really hear and understand what he or she is saying. Evaluate what was said and make your own assessment for taking action. The objective of any communication is to obtain a desired response. Be clear about the response you expect from any communication. For achieving this objective each message needs to be understood. Communication builds understanding. Two angry people yelling and fighting may hear each other's words but they are not communicating or making any attempts to understand one another.

Keep your communication simple and clear by thinking straight. Muddled thinking leads to muddled communication. Be clear about what you mean. Come straight to the point. Good communicators do not beat about the bush and waste words. The more words you use to make a point the more confusion you may cause. Be yourself. Be real. You will be more convincing and more comfortable if you act according to your nature. Only if you work well do you have any right to complain. Tit-for-tat is not the best policy either as a long term or even as a short-term solution for settling scores. The best way to settle scores is by excelling in whatever you are engaged in. In the Indian market the demand for jobs is limited and the supply is more. This situation is likely to continue for a long time to come. Even for the existing personnel it is important to upgrade their knowledge and skills so that there is no gap between their knowledge and changing job requirements in view of the latest technological developments. A high level of competence and skills will always have a market and a demand. Do not be brutal with your team. It can be counter-productive. Have faith in your people and keep on reinforcing their goals. Be lavish in recognizing and appreciating the contributions of others. Always be on the look out to revise your goals and targets and push them forwards.

★ Be yourself.
Be real

How To Negotiate Successfully

The secret of successful negotiation is, first, to be clear in your mind as to what you are negotiating. Identification of the problem is of utmost importance. It is also best to anticipate the expected outcome. Sometimes the negotiations get bogged down as the people involved do not agree as to what is the real problem. Each person wants his version of the problem to be accepted. Some discussion is always desirable and needed before the two sides can carry on with the negotiation. The idea behind this is that the subject should be clear to all negotiating sides. The common saying that they each needs to be 'on the same page' is very much applicable during negotiations. The next step in the process of negotiation is to take the opinion of the others and only then move ahead. The other person should reflect or restate the opinion as he heard and understood it. Then in all fairness you have to take turns and state your opinion. Just because you are thinking about the other person's opinion does not mean that you agree with it. At this stage in the negotiation you are simply acting as a mirror. This is being done for more clarity and more understanding. There are bound to be differences in any negotiations. Some times brainstorming ideas for the solution pays. During the brainstorming the negotiating parties are expected to place their ideas and possible solutions on the table for the consideration of others. During such a session it is important to realize that this is not a time for discussion or judgement. This is simply an idea-gathering occasion.

It is best to lay down a rule with the consent of all concerned before the negotiations start that all ideas will be respected whether both parties agree with them or not. It is tremendously helpful to write down the ideas in a notebook or on a board. When all possible ideas have been written down then it is time to consider all of them and decide which is the most workable idea. Discuss each idea until you select the best one. It is best to clarify the details about the performance of any particular job. Understanding needs to be specific and defined in behavioural and performance terms. A deadline should be decided on before which the idea can be tried out. Problems which may arise should be anticipated. It is also best to assess after a reasonable amount of time how any contract or understanding has worked on the ground. The good points and the points which need to be altered or changed should be noted for future reference. Keep in view the mechanics of working so that any alteration should not mean re-doing the job again.

The most important step in solving any difficulty is identifying the problem or problems faced. It is a challenge which needs to be met clearly and squarely. Looking for problems and solving them may sometimes mean reviewing the past. This will add to the win-win feeling. Life is a series of compromises and this is what it is all about. Being more assertive and speaking up for oneself are confidence-creating actions and bring about better personal relationships, increased satisfaction at work and often the ability to negotiate for better situations or emoluments. Best results emerge when each person feels that he is a winner. Each person should have a feeling of having got something of what he wants or had planned to get.

It is normal in any organization for some people to carry tales against their friends, colleagues or partners. Stabbing in the back is not something new. It is better to identify and know about people who do this. The best course is to keep such persons at a distance without compromising your dignity or competence. Co-operation does not mean that you share every single thought about everything with everybody. Think before you discuss anything with anybody. Nine times out of ten it will be recycled and repeated with exaggerated emphasis. Be sure of one thing that if you say something uncomplimentary it will be relayed back to the person concerned in due course of time. Quite often some organizations consider gossip a source of information. You have to devise your own methods and organise your own defences against the attacks by backbiters. Perform your best so that when the organization evaluates you against the pre-determined standards you come out with flying colours.

You should not hesitate to confront the scandalmonger or tale-carrier. Present him all the evidence you have in a calm, measured manner. He may realize that his game is up and may possibly not trouble you again. Such a person cowers before his superiors and bullies and attacks his colleagues. It is better to let him know that you are aware of his doings. Let him know that you would confront him headon. You should practice calm and be in control of the situation when having a showdown with such a person. Always remember that most people including your friends and colleagues will be happy to see you pulled down rather than pulled up towards success. You have to protect your reputation and think of strategies of dealing with such people.

> ★ Never hesitate to ask for clarification if you have failed to grasp the other's point of view.

Whatever be your job, effective communication is a must for success. There are no hard and fast rules for effective communication. Always plan and think ahead about what you are going to say. It is preferable to write down what you want to say so that no points are left out and there are no loose ends. Simple sentences, phrases and words should be used so that the listener has no difficulty in comprehending what the communicator wants to convey. Prepare yourself and become master of your subject by increasing your professional competence in every possible way. Enhance your knowledge on all subjects related to your job or profession. Prepare yourself thoroughly on the subject you are going to speak. The same applies for writing on any subject. Clear and audible speech is more effective than any garbled communication. Hence, there is a premium on speaking clearly and audibly. When giving instructions, check twice with the person charged with the duty of carrying them out or with the listener whether he has understood accurately and completely what is required of him. Interruptions are a part of any interaction or communication. In case of prolonged interruptions, always re-establish the link. Do a little bit of recapitulation, if necessary, of what has been already said. Always pay undivided attention while listening to any speaker as it makes for perfect understanding. Sometimes a speaker may have a boring way of putting across ideas. While listening always make notes of what the speakers are saying. It will keep you active, awake and will enable you to recall what was said whenever any action is called for. Never hesitate to ask for clarification if you have failed to grasp the other's point of view. If it is a discussion, repeat what the speaker has said to check whether what he has said has been correctly understood or not. It makes the discussion and communication meaningful. For good and meaningful communication it is always better not to react instantly and mutter something in anger to avoid any possible regrets later on. Using jargon, technical terms and terminology is not always the best strategy when speaking to a mixed or a non-specialized audience. Such a speech or exposition is not always understood by the listeners. It is better to speak as if you are speaking to the layman. Do not speak too fast, too slow or softly when speaking in noisy surroundings. If you do so, chances are that you will neither be heard nor understood. It is best to assume that everybody may not understand you. Hence use simple language. Do not distract yourself by looking around too much as it may affect your flow of thoughts and speech. When listening, do not jump to a hasty conclusion that you have understood everything. Wait till the other person has finished speaking. Half listening is as good as not listening.

What People Expect

Be responsive when problems arise. Make all efforts to prevent a communication breakdown during a crisis. Concentrate on facing the difficulties and finding solutions. Be prepared to talk about them in detail only with a view to overcoming the crisis. Go all out to find solutions, if necessary aggressively, so that your operation success does not get unstuck. Before people draw adverse conclusions about the situation, talk about it voluntarily

> Remembering names is an indication that you are interested in others.

in a manner that is quick and complete. Let those most directly affected know that every possible step is being taken to meet their difficulties. When faced with an organizational or business problem keep the people most directly affected in the picture until the problem is thoroughly explained or resolved. If you respect and seek to work with those who oppose you, you are bound to earn the respect of even your adversaries. If a spokesman is required for explaining any situation, the seniormost executive concerned should be prepared to brief others on any significant event or delegate a person well-conversant with it to do so. It is important to analyze the impact of any crisis affecting the organization and inform and alert the concerned individuals or teams. Real integrity is to acknowledge the reality of the situation promptly and take remedial steps. Be true to your organizational commitment and personal conscience by exhibiting concern, sympathy, or remorse or whatever the case may require. While dealing with a crisis, go beyond what is expected or required of you. Learn from your mistakes. Keep in mind all the time what you have learned. Commit yourself to preventing errors and problems from arising again. You do not have to settle for the first draft of anything. You should work hard to make it your own document rather than somebody else's.

A number of people have problems in remembering names. It can be embarrassing and sometimes potentially career-busting if you forget the name of your clients or your seniors when you are about to make introductions at an important gathering. The art of remembering names is not just a learned skill. It can give you a competitive plus. Positive images and impressions are very valuable. Remembering names is an indication that you are interested in others. Forgetting names gives the opposite impression. When being introduced, listen to the names carefully. Quickly and quietly repeat the names to yourself. It will be still better if you immediately use it in your conversation for example, "It has been nice meeting you, Mr Om Prakash."

If you come across an unusual name, ask for its spelling

with appropriate politeness. Find out if the name has anything unusual about it. Apart from the fact that it flatters the person concerned it will enable you remember his or her name. Link an easy to remember activity or an association with a name. One technique can be to connect a new acquaintance with an activity like a morning walk or a business or profession. Keep on reinforcing your memory by frequently using the person's name in your conversation. If this does not work, then ask for the spelling of the name and write it down and use it in your conversation with others. Never belittle compliments that you receive as they are something which others may be genuinely feeling about you. Minimizing compliments belittles both you and the person offering the compliment. When you are complimented, just say, "Thank you." You will find that it works wonders. Always sound positive as a doer who will and can be counted on to get the assigned job done. Use positive phrases like "I will" as often as possible instead of "I will try".

Be specific in your commitments and honour them. Your positive attitude and choice of words will not only influence others but also strongly motivate you to get the job done.

Very often a person may be waiting to see you while you are talking to somebody on the phone or are in the middle of a conversation with someone else. Acknowledge the person's presence with a wave of hand, a smile or a nod. The other person will get the message that you know that he is waiting for you and you will attend to him shortly. It is a simple gesture which if not extended makes the other person feel insignificant. Do not use the excuse that you have been busy when reminded that you had promised to do something by a certain date and time. It only shows that you have given a low priority to the request.

How To Succeed In An Interview

An interview is a meeting between two persons for the purpose of getting a view of each other or for knowing each other. The word 'interview' in simple English means 'view between' or 'sight between' the two persons. The person being interviewed is generally being assessed for his suitability for a particular assignment. An interview is a process that involves interaction between two persons. Sometimes more than one person or a number of interviewers interact with a candidate to check the interviewee's suitability and ability to deliver goods for a particular assignment. Interviews are generally held for employment either at the initial level or for higher assignments either in the same organization or a different one. Interviews generally focus on assessing the personal and professional background of the candidate, his educational and work experiences, his interests, hobbies, his family, friends, his personal habits, views and attitudes to a job, life or work. It is best to be fresh when going for an interview. Do not study or stay up late in the night or attend a late night party a day before the interview. Go for the interview in the best of moods.

★ A candidate should keep a cool head and be relaxed throughout the interview.

Make sure a day before the interview that the dress you want to wear for the interview is clean and ironed. It should be appropriate and understated. The last minute discovery of a missing button or a frayed dress can lead to a lot of nervousness. A standby dress should also be kept ready. It should be neither gaudy nor flashy. If any testimonials or certificates, marksheets or other relevant papers are required these should be separately kept in an interview folder along with the interview call letter on top of the file. The candidate should prepare himself well for answering any likely questions which will generally be based on the resumé or job experience of the candidate. On the day of the interview the candidate should reach the venue well before time. It is best to reach at least 25 minutes in advance. It will help the candidate to relax and feel comfortable with the environment. It is wise to make allowance for traffic jams or any other contingency. It is best to read as many newspapers as possible on the day of the interview. If the job is in the economic sphere, it is best to read the economic newspapers not only on the day of the interview but also a week in advance. Be aware of the important happenings in the country as well as in the world. While waiting to be called in, the candidate should observe the surroundings and interact with the other candidates for getting any useful information.

While answering questions, the interviewee should not launch into lengthy replies where short answers would do. It is important to remember that the interviewer is testing a candidate for knowledge or experience. Preferably, no answers should be given in monosyllables. A candidate should keep a cool head and be relaxed throughout the interview. If there is a question to which a candidate does not have any answer, it is best to admit it instead of bluffing. Any lies will lead to further questions. These may expose a candidate as a liar and show him in a bad light thus ruining all his chances for success.

The person being interviewed should be comfortable and relaxed. As much as the interviewee needs the job the interviewers also need suitable candidates for making their organization achieve its goals. So the mutual needs are almost equal though interviewers have a slight edge.

During the interview every question should be answered with clarity and confidence even if some odd or difficult questions are asked. The interviewee should be attentive and alert throughout the interview. It is not a difficult or an impossible demand as generally no interview lasts for more than 30 minutes. The interviewee should be a good listener so that he understands at once what is being asked. It is best to remember that a candidate is not being tested for his knowledge of the *Encyclopaedia Britannica*. So, no interviewer is going to ask impossible questions. The interview process is a technique to explore and analyze human behaviour. It involves a step-by-step process generally covering the following stages.

Selection And Intimation For Interview

It is generally based on the requirements of an organization. The selection of the candidates is done according to the parameters which indicate the area of consideration. An interview assesses and explores the personal and professional background of a candidate as well as analyzes the psychological make-up of the candidate. The candidates should attempt to create a positive first impression. The interview board or the single interviewer will generally initiate the interview. The biodata, the interests, hobbies, academic qualifications or professional competence and general awareness are generally the starting point of an interview. A candidate should prepare in advance exactly what he or she would like to say about his family and himself. It should be brief and to the point. It should carry a positive note. The candidate should not start a dissertation on the family history. When summoned for interview in the interview chamber, the candidate should not forget to ask permission before entering the interview room. He should not sit down unless asked to do so. The candidate should not speak too fast or in a garbled tone. The candidate should be his natural self and not make any artificial gestures. The candidate should not interrupt if the board members are talking. He or she should not begin answering before the interviewer has completed the question, nor pick up and fiddle with objects like paperweights or other objects lying on the table. He should sit upright and not slouch during the interview. The candidate should keep his hands in control and avoid gesticulations or emotional outbursts. While answering questions the candidate should not change his stand. If a candidate can find some good reason to do so, then he or she can praise the interviewer. But it should not be overdone giving an impression of outright flattery. After the interview is over, the candidate should not extend his or her hand for a handshake unless the interviewer extends it first. The candidate should close the door behind him when leaving.

If the interview is for a professional job, the interviewee should start from his qualifications and go on to work experience. In case the candidate does not have work experience he could talk about any project done or any position held in school or college. To tackle such questions the candidate should establish a co-relation between them and his subject. The candidate should explain the practical applicability of his work and how it could help in the job for which he is being interviewed. The interviewer in many cases is on the look out for analyzing the psychological make-up of the candidate through his conduct, behaviour and deportment during the interview. The personality and attitude of a candidate plays a vital role in the success of his interview. The body language of a candidate is a reflection of his whole personality. Body language includes facial expressions, arm, hand and leg movements. Body language also includes the attitude towards work and life. An experienced interviewer can assess a candidate for positive or negative attitudes, integrity, loyalty, creativity and other inter-personal interaction skills through body language. If a candidate puts his best foot forward, he is bound to get the best results.

Public Speaking

Pick up your audiences if you can so that your presentation is relevant to your job or what you know. This is the only way to move up faster in the world of public speaking. However, it is not always possible to have everything to your liking. A beginner may have to experience different types of audiences. Once you gain experience in speaking and develop a reputation as a good orator the size and type of audiences grow bigger, different and higher. When you cannot handle a situation or speak on a subject relevant to the topic on hand make it a point to say: 'No'.

Do not accept every request to give a talk even if you are available. Pick up your engagements and present yourself in a way which indicates the greatest chance of success. You have to suit your speech to the audience and also in the language they can understand. A technical presentation before a non-technical audience is the most ill-advised thing to do. A subject has to be tailored to meet the level and requirements of the audience. Never accept any engagement to address an audience which does not match your abilities, inclinations, likes and dislikes. Push your abilities to the limit in whatever area you are to perform. Never undertake to do anything which you cannot do well.

Use humorous material to make your presentation interesting. Each joke should flow naturally from and into the subject. Memorize what you have to say. Become less dependent on a written presentation and this will automatically raise your credibility. This approach will give an impression to the audience that you really know your job and are thorough in your subject and are fully prepared. It also enables you to build a rapport with your audience and get closer to them. The closer you are to them the better they will receive your ideas. It is better to talk naturally to the audience rather than read to them. An audience would not like jokes read out to them. Using humour in presentations will make you more likeable and effective and will build a great rapport with the audience. With properly spaced humour and facts there is likely to be less resistance to any message you want to convey to the people.

> Using humour will help you connect with an audience.

Being an expert in your field and able to reel off hours and hours of information on the relevant topic is different from being an effective speaker. Business executives and political leaders have realized the potential of humour for a successful talk or presentation. Humour adds a lively tone to any talk. Using humour and other techniques adds a fine polish to your presentation skills. This can make you stand out in a crowd.

Using humour will help you connect with an audience. It prevents boredom, arouses interest of the audience and keeps their attention focused on the point you want to make. It will enable you to emphasize your points and ideas. Humour also disarms hostility. In case of any flattering introduction you can use it to put the things in proper perspective. You can also use humour to get your point across without creating any cynicism. Facts and figures with a touch of humour can make a positive impression and information given more memorable. It lightens the burden of seriousness and gloom in life and spreads cheerfulness all round. It also brightens up others' lives and opens a whole new world for many others.

Your Resumé Is Your Mirror

The importance of making a good resumé cannot be underestimated while applying for a position. People in authority would like to know whether you fulfil their requirements or not for a particular assignment. Resumés are vital to any job hunting. It is the most important tool which can help you in getting a job of your choice. The importance of making a good resumé should not be underrated. The main objective of a resumé is to generate the interest of

> You can only sell yourself by highlighting your strengths.

a potential employer to interview you. It can be a complete, concise, clearly stated summary of your competence, experience, activities, education, personal qualities, skills and background. Matching the job requirements with your capabilities needs to be reflected in your resumé. This information is essential to highlight your background and competence for potential employers. More than one resumé with a different emphasis may be required depending upon the job you are aiming to secure. However, it is essential for an eye-catching resumé to be concise, readable and catchy. List your experience, employment record, work history, positions held, appointments, skill, qualifications, accomplishments, strengths, education, affiliations, publications, papers, honours, personal and additional references and anything else with specific reference to the job applied. The resumé should contain crucial information which should tempt potential employers to hire you and your strongest points should be highlighted.

Do not be contradictory. Be consistent. Choose a pattern and an order of information, presentation or a format of highlighting the points you want to be noted particularly. Never lie about your competence. Sooner or later you will be found out and you may be sacked unceremoniously. If you are giving previous experience in the resumé, do not lie about dates, work history, skills and abilities, descriptions of jobs held, education or anything else. Your past job history, performance, education skills, and salary are all verifiable factors. If you exaggerate your competence and skills and get a job on the basis of false information, chances are that your real worth will be discovered sooner than you expect. It is best to be honest.

Sometimes the objective statement is the most difficult part of a resumé. The best course would be to write your objective statement at the end. Mention your qualifications in order of relevance from most to least. List your degree and educational qualifications to begin with if they are relevant to the job which you are applying for. Give dates of previous employment in the resumé. Without dates it may seem like that you have something to conceal. Include your hobbies and interests as they reveal a lot about you. Have a trusted friend to scrutinize the final draft of your resumé and check details as well as style of presentation and give an honest and objective opinion about it with suggestions for improvement. Seriously consider any advice given on your resumé by your sincere well-wishers. Get a second or third and even a fourth opinion if you feel it is needed. It is your advertisement and your selling point. You can only sell yourself by highlighting your strengths. If you want to add something which does not fit into any existing parameters of your resumé list it as an additional segment.

Searching For Greener Pastures

Many times people do job hunting for better jobs while still employed. Searching for a new job can result in your getting fired as no employer wants an employee who is not giving his best and is instead planning to leave for some other assignment. The following suggestions minimize such risks. Respect your duty hours though searching for a new job may involve having to be away from the office for personally applying and attending the interviews. Use your

★
> Good human relations should take precedence over everything else.

leave or holidays for such work. Do not pretend to be sick for this purpose. Never give your prospective employers your present office phone number. Use your home phone and attach an answering machine to it so that you can get messages even when you are away from your home or are away to the office. Be discreet. Do not broadcast that you are looking for another job. If you get a new job inform your superior immediately. Try to leave the present organization on a pleasant note. Some people use the new job offer for negotiating a higher counter offer from their present employer. This is not a correct strategy as once you give a commitment to join the new assignment you must honour it.

Everybody in life wants to go higher and higher and increase his chances for promotion. There is nothing wrong with being ambitious and in wanting to go ahead. Make sure you want it and work for promotion. Set your own objectives and increase your competence. Goals are and should be treated as deadlines to give a sense of urgency. Respect the chain of command and hierarchy. Your own prospects are linked to your organization's success. Be sure that your objectives are no different from those of your organization. People working in the same organization as you would rather work for the success of the organization rather than yours. In fact, most people will resist working for you to enable you to succeed. Generally, beware of such people. Make a list of those with whom you have a neutral or even a negative relationship. Your approach should be to win them over by taking genuine interest in them. Offer such people help in the area of your strength. To please them you can ask for help in the area of their expertise.

Good human relations should take precedence over everything else. They can smoothen any rough edges. Keep up your enthusiasm for your work whatever it may be or wherever it may be. Everybody faces problems. It will help a great deal if you make a hit list of five or six of your major problems. One of the biggest problems is that of wastage of time. Identify at least eight big time-gobblers. Keep them under a scanner and review them frequently so that you can try to eliminate as many as you can. Everybody has some level of dissatisfaction even with the best of jobs. The ideal approach is to work on a solution before changing a job. There is no guarantee that in your next job you will be fully satisfied or happy or that it will be any better than the present one. In the event of your deciding to take up another job, be clear in your objective as to why you are seeking a change Also, ask yourself as to how you will give a better performance and how you will handle it after getting it. Be brutally frank and honest with yourself about your competence, abilities, skills and potential. Have a systematic plan. Be clear in your mind about it. Never be argumentative. Try always for a compromise. Be sure that you and your future employers understand each other. Once you have agreed upon a solution, do everything to advance it. Become competent and acquire the necessary skills. Changes do take time. You have to prepare yourself for the same. List questions and be ready with their answers. Build a strong network and list all the people you know who are in good positions. Be in touch with them. At the same time keep your professional skills updated. Try to

> ★ Keep communications short, concise, simple, interesting and focused.

learn something new everyday. Keep your finances in order. Determine how long you can afford to have the present lifestyle without any regular income from any job. Continue taking steps to extend that period so that you know that one day when you retire and will have to fall back upon your savings or pension, you will not be caught unawares. In any job prove your worth by getting involved and learning your work inside out. Expand your networks. If you find that your colleagues and bosses are not helping, try to get help from other sources. Always be on the move. If you decide to leave a job, line up another one before you do. Always keep yourself alert, productive and positive. Make your skills suited for your current job. Keep on striving for more effectiveness and efficiency.

It is only for your competence that you will be respected by your peers and higher-ups. Always evaluate your choices before you burn your bridges. Always be conscious of what your organization and your peers expect of you and how you can improve communication with them. If somebody compliments you do not deflect it as deflecting a compliment often draws unwanted attention. Follow the methods of doers as it is only the doers who can be counted on to get anything done.

Keep communications short, concise, simple, interesting and focused. Do not forget the basic objectives of communication and the message you want to convey. Delete everything irrelevant to your objective. Never apologize on the way of your functioning or presentation. Always give an impression of being an expert. Using words like: 'I think', 'I feel' or 'I apprehend' convey an uncertainty. Use language which indicates action. Prepare yourself thoroughly. Be honest and if you do not know something say so. Do not tell lies. Be attentive when others speak and ask questions if you do not understand anything.

Ask And You Will Receive

Many people feel frustrated as they are unable to get what they need or want. Sometimes not getting what you want is due to the fact that you do not ask for it. Sometimes even after making many attempts or requests people still do not get what they want. This is happening in all types of relationships all the time. This includes intimate relationships, family friendships and work relationships. The following tips will help you get what you want in any relationship. These tips are not manipulations. Most of the time in intimate or other kinds of relationships people are reluctant to ask for what they want. The first tip to remember is that you have the right to ask for anything you need or want. Always ask for help or anything what you want from anyone you want it from.

> ★ Everybody likes the freedom and power of being able to truly choose.

Do not presume that the other person knows your mind or your requirements. People like to be requested. Of course you should be ready to hear a 'Yes' or a 'No'. Frame your requests in such a way that you are prepared to hear either a 'Yes' or a 'No' without feeling bad. Frame your question or requests in such a way that you are more likely to hear a 'Yes' than a 'No'. At the same time give the person requested a choice. Everybody likes the freedom and power of being able to truly choose. It is best to be gracious if you get a 'No' to your request. An ungracious reaction will show that you were making a demand and not a request. Nobody likes to be bullied and hence demands are seldom positively responded to. Demand or coercion is always resisted. Do not make the person saying 'No' feel guilty or in the wrong. This way you will be asking for more refusals. Be gracious and you will get a 'Yes' soon enough.

Every person has the right to make a request. It is also the right of the person requested to say 'No'. You need an alternative strategy if someone says 'No'. You cannot make a person do or give you what you want anyhow. But you can still make sure to get what you want if you assume the person or people who you are asking for something have your best interests in their mind. If you still get a 'No' then you must assume that the reasons for your request were either not convincing or not clear. Presume that if your reasons had been clear and unambiguous your request would have been agreed to. Make your presentation effective and well known next time. Do not nag while making a request. Nagging is a terrible way of making the same request over and over in order to wear out the other person down and literally get out of him what you want. Nagging does not get you what you want. It can backfire as it creates intense anger in both the nagged and the nagger. Small things can and do have a profound effect on us as well as our job performance. Be clear in your mind about the impact of a 'Yes' or 'No' on your life, career and job. Share this information with the person you are asking for a favour from if you think that your trust will not be misused. Life is a give and take affair. If you want to get a 'Yes' and get what you want from the other person you have to be ready to reciprocate. If you give the other person what he or she wants consistently, you will get what you want more often, too. The key is to give and do what you are being requested and not what you think the other person wants.

> ★ Ask for what you want but ask for it politely, delicately and directly.

If you have to repeat a request more than once, do so. When you get a 'Yes' and it helps you in your mission make a big deal out of it. Make the person who favoured you feel good. Appreciation is loved by everybody. The more you appreciate the more the other person will be inclined to agree to your request in future. In fact, even if you do not feel like appreciating make an effort to appreciate. After some time you will begin to feel appreciative. Never hesitate asking someone to do something they themselves should have done. Do not show you are angry. Everybody is different with different standards and priorities. Ask for what you want but ask for it politely, delicately and directly.

6

ATTITUDE IS ALL

Shape Your Life

Challenge yourself to fulfil your dreams. You must keep in view that your attitude is what determines any result or outcome. It depends entirely on you whether you want to be happy or unhappy. It is your attitude which makes you stronger, braver and more capable of success than you ever thought it possible. It is your attitude which determines whether you will give up at the first obstacle or first sign of defeat. This depends solely on each one of us. Do not get bogged down in the belief that it is your circumstances which determine your happiness. It is up to each one of us to make a conscious choice of either being angry about our circumstances or using our energy for a positive change. All of us have to face good and bad situations in life but it is only we who can overcome the same if we persevere. Blaming life and difficult circumstances for our unhappiness does not solve any problem. It is only taking the easy way out. Commit yourself to learning from your mistakes. Learn lessons and apply them for bettering your life. Be committed to getting up each and every time when you fall and when things do not work out to your satisfaction and expectation. 'Try and try again', should be the motto of all those who want the best in life. Tiredness and disillusionment should have no place in your life till you have achieved what you have set out to achieve. Each one of us has an inalienable right to success.

Never let hope die as in that case your spirit will also collapse and you will lose the will and desire to be happy. Never allow mistakes or misfortunes to become an excuse to look at life with an 'I'm such a loser' mentality. This approach generates a toxic point of view. It wrecks not only your self-esteem but your chances for happiness as well. Keep things in proper perspective. Be bold to change your life for the better. A happy person is one who has no cares at all; a cheerful person may have cares but he does not let them get him down. Have the courage to rise up against heavy odds every time you fall. See yourself as a brave and strong person. Identify the fears you need to face and overcome. This is the only way in which you will be encouraging yourself to see yourself in a more positive light. Never use your mistakes or misfortunes as an excuse or as a justification for not making your life what you want it to be.

Be Yourself

It is important to be aware of how you behave when things do not work out as you had planned or hoped. Reactions of individuals vary from screaming, crying, raving and ranting to overeating or sulking. Be conscious of the degree you allow your emotions to control you. Also check up whether at that time you choose to keep your values and ethics in focus or not. It is normal to give vent to one's feelings but make sure that you do not waste all your time in expressing your emotions. Be always

> Practice looking for and focusing on the positive side of even the most adverse of situations.

working towards the solution to the problems you face or for coping with the situation. Developing a positive attitude in the midst of difficulties is a learned skill. Practice looking for and focusing on the positive side of even the most adverse of situations. Visualize a brighter better future and a glorious life. Find happiness options in the midst of difficult circumstances. They will help you to emerge triumphant. Whether you go up or down it is up to you. It all depends on what you choose to become by focusing on the things which matter to you, your life and your profession. Sometimes for days we wrestle with a problem from every angle. Still we are far from finding a solution. All efforts of concentrating on the problem, working out permutations and combinations and even help from colleagues do not help and no solution is visible. You feel that all your theories seem to have fallen through and you are about to admit defeat. Then suddenly the right answer occurs often in the most improbable settings like during your morning walk or bath. Sometimes the best answers enter your mind just when you are no longer focused on the problem. It is the result of concentrating on a problem and the mind churning up a solution.

You should never sacrifice your self-respect. If you believe that people like you or accept you only for what you can do for them then you need to devise new ways of reclaiming your self-respect. Do not lower yourself, slight yourself or put up with wrong things in the hope of gaining someone's approval or friendship. Nobody can take advantage of you unless you allow them to do so. Protect, cherish, and nourish your self-esteem. Believe that you have a personality of your own and you matter for what you are. Never twist your self-esteem into knots in order to be loved and accepted. Besides a one-sided love or friendship that is based on one party being a doormat is not worth anything. In any case it is not true love or friendship. Believe that you deserve the best. Do not settle for less than the best.

How Your Attitude Rates You

A critical success factor in our lives is the right mental attitude. Just how important is attitude? A study by Harvard University showed that 85% of the reasons for success, accomplishments, promotions etc. were because of the attitudes and only 15% because of technical expertise. Not only in our educational set-up but in society itself we seem to have reversed this process. Attitudes do make a great deal of difference. When we have the right attitude, our performance is effective and good results inevitably emerge. We see this time and time again in our everyday life. Business concerns with the right attitudes outperform their status quo

> ★ Be grateful and show your gratitude to others where others have done something for you and obliged you.

believers who are their peers. Right attitudes make all the difference whether dealing with spouses, children, parents, friends, superiors, subordinates or co-workers. They help us to win in any and every situation in life.

The next question which arises is as to what can be done to improve our attitudes. The first step is by increasing our enthusiasm which in turn creates a positive attitude. Enthusiasm or lack of it is visible in everything we do and say. The right attitude is greatly affected by our level of enthusiasm. Talk only about positive and good things with your friends and family. Encourage your children and all the people you come in contact. Praise people as often as you can. Be altruistic and helpful. Lavish appreciation for genuine achievement. Compliments are both easy to give and easy not to give. Most of the time we quickly recognize and praise big accomplishments. The little things which are done well are not even noticed. In fact, sometimes they are even more important. It will be a good idea for harmonious and smooth relationships to develop the habit of noticing and commenting on appearances, ideas, efforts and routine tasks that have been well done. Be grateful and show your gratitude to others where others have done something for you and obliged you.

Being enthusiastic will change your attitude. It will also change the perception and approach of others. A positive attitude is both infectious and contagious. We must choose carefully the people we come in contact with. We should be equally careful in surrounding ourselves with only positive people. We should also be conscious as to how our own attitude is affecting people around us. Our effort should be directed towards being a positive role model with a vibrant and an enthusiastic attitude. This will not only profoundly affect our own success and well-being but those of others, too, with whom we come in contact. Always be smiling with your eyes, your gestures, posture and conversation. Instead of plodding through the day make a conscious effort to be more upbeat. Make others feel important. Be truly interested in what others have to communicate. Our interest in others sends them the message that what they have to say is important and we are all ears for it. This approach will win us many admirers and friends. It will also reduce resistance to your quest for success. For this each one of us needs to improve his listening skills. Our attitude should be to build people up so they can honestly feel better for having talked to you.

Always be on the look out to do something for others. Keep giving both in big and small ways. Volunteer your time to guide others even if it is one hour per month. Do something for yourself. No matter how busy you are never ignore yourself. Take time out for yourself everyday. Enjoy the simple pleasures of reading a book or watching birds. Indulge yourself by doing something you have always wanted to do like watching a movie or roaming about in the market. I personally miss no opportunity to do window shopping for hours together whether in India or abroad. Forgive others as grudges and grievances are unhealthy emotional baggage. Let go of them so that you can get on with the main task of your life. Do not be overtly critical of yourselves. Self-flagellation is both unhealthy and detrimental. Do the best you can and then be satisfied

★ Life is happening right now.

that you have done your best. It is essential to know what is really important and who matters. Ask yourself whether the way you are living your life is consistent with what you regard is important to you. Also, ask yourself whether you are concentrating on what matters most in your life. If you are on the wrong track, then take action to determine how to get from where you are to where you want to be. Gift yourself happiness which is a choice. It is available to everyone through the right attitude. Take the approach from 'achieving to be happy' to 'happily achieving'.

It is a fact that we cannot change the past, however hard we try but we can certainly learn from the past. Based on past experience we can definitely do things now that will affect, shape and change our future. Life is happening right now. It is important to focus on today both in our personal and professional life. It is immeasurably important to end each day thinking that we have done our best. This will prevent day-dreaming and living in the future. We should be living each day as though our life, success and happiness depends on it. Here are a few things that each one of us can do to make our life a masterpiece.

At the beginning of each day (or the night before) ask yourself as to what is the single most important thing that I can do today to make my life a masterpiece of motivation and achievement? Whatever be your answer, make sure that you focus on it throughout the day. In actual life most of us would fumble. But this can be overcome by practice.

At the end of the day ask yourself the following questions: Did I do my best today in everything I did? Also, ask yourself as to what is on the credit side on the one hand and on the other what is on the debit side in your life and work. Finding answers to the above questions will give you a recipe for discovering and appreciating the things in your life that are going well. It will also clarify as to where you have fallen short of the objectives and where more efforts are needed. By securing answers to the above questions you will begin to discover patterns where some activities have produced desired results and others have not. This will enable you to duplicate your successes and eliminate those methods or approaches that did not produce the desired results. It is important to bear in mind that we inevitably attract into our life people and circumstances in harmony with our dominant thoughts. Do not think of changing the world but think of changing yourself. Do not aim for easy targets. This is not the way to grow. Go where the expectations and the demands to perform are the highest. For success and leadership it is important to remember that a person who wants to lead an orchestra has to have his back to the crowd. Learn to use your personal power to create an extraordinary life. Embrace life as it comes. Focus on this day. This is the only day you can control. If you do so, you will make it a masterpiece of living in harmony with others.

> Do not get nervous when you face any difficulty.

Attitudes To Reach The Top

Your attitude and confidence level carries you forward or backward. It is the attitude that matters. It is as important as your expertise or knowledge. Don't ever let negative feelings overtake you or come near you. Always say to yourself, "I shall do my best and succeed." Any negative suggestions adversely affect attitudes. Remind yourself that if you do not succeed for the first time it is not the end of life. Pressures and expectations sometimes tempt you to adopt unfair means. Keep in mind that, occasionally, it is natural to fail in any venture but never as a human being. A right approach with the right attitude and a strong value system will ultimately lead you to success and your goal. Just having the right attitude and following certain Do's and Don'ts will enable you to come out a winner. Always stay calm and make yourself comfortable when deciding to tackle any problem. Study your problem carefully before attempting to overcome it. Attempt the easier part first. It will give you confidence to tackle the difficult part. There is no negative marking for dealing with the easier portion first. Try to set a time limit for tackling and solving any problem.

Deep breathing and periodic stretching exercises help in relieving stress and tension. Do not get nervous when you face any difficulty. You can win and overcome any problem if you believe you can. Success starts in the mind. Your own assessment of your ability leads you either to success or failure. "Men are born to succeed not to fail," said Henry Thoreau. Faith in yourself and in what you are doing is fundamental to your success. The supreme secret of success is faith, the 'can do' attitude. In other words, that which you constantly think about is likely to happen. Unlike most people, successful people develop a capacity to perceive possibilities even when things seem impossible. An excellent example is the development of the Polaroid instant photograph camera. One day when Edwin H. Land was taking a photograph of his young daughter she asked him why they had to wait to see the pictures. It might appear a naive question to most of us. But it interested her father. It started a serious chain of thought. His reasoning was that when somebody buys a pair of trousers or a car or any other product he can use it straightaway. Why should it be any different in photography? Six months after his daughter's ingenuous question the first 60-second Polaroid camera was not only invented but also went on sale in the USA.

Self-confidence and competence usually go together, though they are different qualities. Belief about one's capabilities strongly governs the level of a person's performance and strengthens his self-confidence. Observing competent and successful people and the way they work is extremely helpful in strengthening self-confidence. Commendation from those we respect that we are doing well is always highly inspiring. Social approval helps us to believe in ourselves. Being in situations in which we are more likely to succeed than fail is itself morale boosting. You should always be challenging yourself to learn and grow. Placing yourself in a situation where there is a high possibility of failure does not add to self-confidence. Try to structure the conditions for success by gradually raising the levels of difficulty in problems. Surround yourselves with supportive individuals.

Most people view any change as a personal threat. They feel that what they are doing now is adequate and fine. Some will recall problems from a previous change. There is always resistance to learning new ways of doing things. There is also a fear of failing in a new environment. Such reactions act as barriers. View such conflicts as distinct challenges. Manage conflicts with yourself and your team. Do not look for patterns that are not really there and magnify the problem. Strip away any possible antagonism. Minimize the factors of the conflict. This should be done by focusing on a positive outcome. Do not always be on an ego trip that you are right. Your approach should be positive. Instead of saying, "I don't think that's smart," or saying, "I don't agree," say, "As we both want the same result any approach that yields results is fine with me." Avoid personal attacks on anybody for their particular beliefs. Analyze the facts. Avoid any head-on conflicts. Never be sarcastic. Even if something goes wrong, try to understand what happened and why. You need not worry about who did it. Never play the role of an inquisitor who asks questions such as, "Why didn't you take care of this months ago?" Or give comments like, "Only one solution makes any sense." Also do not become a storyteller who looks backwards and says: "When we ran into a situation like this two years ago here's what we did." Do not use statements like: "How many times must I tell you not to do that?" Such approaches can be counter-productive and demoralizing. Nobody remains a boss forever.

It is only human that your mood swings, your joys and sorrows and your attitude at home largely depend on your boss's whims and fancies. Prepare the ground for a comfortable working relationship. At work keep your communication with your boss, colleagues and subordinates on a professional level. Do not encourage or bring personal problems to play in these relationships. Do not discuss your family matters with your boss or others. Discourage others from involving you in their personal or family matters. Be up-to-date and competent in your work. Keep the boss updated on a weekly or daily basis or within a time frame mutually agreed upon. Be always positive and polite. If you cannot get something done in the expected and given time inform your boss about it. Get him to rely on you for your sheer professionalism and dedication to the job. If the boss wants some inputs then collect the data. Assimilate the facts and put them down in a coherent and intelligent way. Avoid confrontation as it never pays. Your boss may find fault with you for what you perceive as an unfair accusation. Do not get provoked and react unreasonably. Put your thoughts down on paper. A day later read your views again for a dispassionate assessment.

If you have a different point of view or you wish to deal with some matters in a way entirely opposite to what your boss wants to, then initiate a discussion and be ready to agree or disagree. It is better to defer to your boss in important matters as he has a fuller picture of the entire scenario than a person at a junior level. It is wise to develop a channel of communication with the top management as part of your survival kit. Always keep in view that your boss can never be your best friend.

> ★ Constant and clear communication is the key to successful management.

Nothing is more important in war than unity in command. It is equally true of a business. When a business is small it has limited goals. It is easier if one person exercises authority and gives direction to everything. As an enterprise grows bigger the issues get bigger and intermediate goals multiply. At that stage it becomes important to delegate some decision-making to other people so that they can achieve them for the organization. It is equally important to let such people achieve the set goals in their own way without interference.

Responsibility and authority should normally go together. There can be only one person in charge of one thing at one time. He should have full authority and responsibility to achieve the goals in his own way. This is the only way to keep your objectives in focus. Never divert resources or attention away from the main business. It is not by long speeches that people become brave in times of war. Veterans hardly listen to them. Recruits forget them at the first bullet. Speeches and arguments are useful only during the course of the campaign both in business and war. They counter false reports and eliminate causes of discontent. Constant and clear communication is the key to successful management. People working for an organization will not know what you want them to do if you do not tell them. Efficient and effective communication lets the employees know what to expect and how to go about achieving the company's goals. It unites the entire organization in action on a day-to-day basis. Praise is a highly valued commodity. Never stint on commendation and appreciation. Above all give your best to any job.

Language Of Success

No course in any life runs in straight lines. Everybody faces a lot of problems. There are bound to be frustrations, sufferings, obstacles, tragedies and ups and downs even in the life of the most successful. There is no way in which anyone can wish them away. Life is a one-way journey from where there is no going back. It is a road on which you can only journey forwards. Occassionally, however, life and its opportunities give a second option to improve upon one's track record. Even those who might be considered as role models have had their quotas of uncertainties, anxieties, fears and disaster.

★ • • • • • • • • • • • •
: Managing your :
: life is your own :
: responsibility. :
• • • • • • • • • • • • •

It is possible to control our lives on the same lines as an expert scientist controls actions so that the reactions are as anticipated. It is a continuous effort to order one's life and keep its pieces in place. One need not be helpless even in the face of adverse circumstances. The only trouble is that we are constantly plagued by uncertainties and apprehensions. The unfamiliar is always strange and brings about its own apprehensions. I was allocated to the Karnataka cadre in 1961. On joining the Indian Police Service, my parents were more apprehensive than I was as to how I will be able to live so far away from them and whether I would get the food I was used to. I, in fact, welcomed the unknown thinking that ultimately everything will turn out well. It was a great cultural and environmental change with totally different food habits and a language which was Greek to me as it would be to any north Indian going to the south for work. I adapted to the change and in fact deemed myself a Kannidaga by domicile. I welcomed the future with a certainty that I had consciously adopted another Indian state and a language which had no similarity either with Punjabi, Hindi, Urdu or English. Worries, concerns and problems have only that much power over us as we allow them. Imaginary happenings and expectations do more damage than any physical happening. If we can prepare and train our minds, we have the strength and capability to transform our limitations into advantages and liabilities into assets. It is up to us make our mind work for us. United there is little a group cannot do. Divided there is little they can do.

It is only by dedication, devotion, hard work and doing our best in whatever we are engaged in that we can achieve great things even though it may seem impossible. It is only in this way that we can generate unlimited powers for achieving any goal that we may wish to achieve.

Mindset controls both our expectations and life. Only when our expectations are not realized that we are filled with tensions, worries and these afflictions affect our happiness. These factors take the joy out of living. No attitude or approach in life is eternal. The worst of habits and practices can be changed with persistence. The mind abhors vacuum. Something will always stick in the mind. Basically all of us appreciate goodness, justice, wisdom, love and fair play.

It is within our own power to decide the kind of life we wish to lead and change any vicious quality or habit like anxiety, uncertainty or passivity. It all depends on the kind of thoughts we allow to enter in our minds. Our thoughts determine our future. Managing your life is your own responsibility. Nobody else can or will do anything for you so that you have a comfortable existence. If anybody could do so, he would prefer to do it for himself rather than for you or me. Hence, the no-blame game will have a positive effect. You could also convince yourself that it was a question of fate and not your own approach if events do not turn out the way you want them.

Hard work leads to appreciation and advancement in your life and profession. For a shirker there are no takers. The outcome of your life depends both upon the hourly and daily choices you make. A positive choice will take you far in life. The negative choice will create circumstances which will lead to your being left behind in the race of life. You have the power to hurt or benefit yourself. It is strange that though we know we can make what we want of life most of us are still left behind. We have to plan, think of things and matters which will do good to us. Thinking is a precursor and a catalyst. Only proper planning leads to all action. The more time you spend on planning and thinking the more you will be able to accomplish.

You should only count on yourself. Never totally depend on others as it will lead to frustrations and disappointment when they do not come up to your expectations. This is the only way in which you can shape your own future and destiny. Nobody will do it for you. People who work only for money are mercenaries. Their objective is to put in a few fixed hours and do the minimum to retain their jobs. It is for this reason that government work which is considered nobody's work is done so shoddily. Good workers are in demand everywhere. A man is not so much a slave to others as he is to his own mindset and inadequacies. We can be the masters of our fate if we resolve to be the captain of our souls and activities. The consequences of our good or bad deeds will generate the results in direct proportion to the inputs.

Honesty with yourself is the best policy as cheating yourself lowers your self-esteem. This is more important than the approval of the world. Self-honesty is a kind of mental hygiene and it is as important as physical hygiene. It does not mean that you should neglect physical hygiene. But mental cleansing and good thoughts are as important as physical cleaning.

The mind is the key factor in maintaining good mental

health and physical well-being. When an unpleasant and debilitating thought of limitation, sickness and ill heath enters your mind, throw it out and replace it by a positive one. Never give way to a negative mental impulse. There is loveliness all around us if we care to see. The mind has unlimited powers within. What the mind of man can conceive, the mind of man can achieve. Achieving any results is possible if you can consciously control and use your mind power.

Never try to ape and imitate. You cannot be but what you are. God has made each individual unique. You cannot be a carbon copy of others. However, you can always learn from the success of others. Successful imitation is possible just as a person mimics others. A mimic is hardly a substitute for the original. A duplicate can accomplish only duplicate tricks. A successful actor or actress like Amitabh Bachchan or Hema Malini or a singer like Lata Manageshkar have hundreds of people like them in the country who can deliver their dialogues or sing the songs they sang as well as them. But a fake is a fake and there are no takers for fakes both in reel and real life. You cannot fake success. Success thrives on hope, courage, competence and respect for time and hard work. Never put off anything you should do now. Do it now. A habit is a good habit which will yield the best dividends. Delay and unhappiness go together. A fictional bright future can be brought about only if we will make our present to be what we want the future to be. Happiness is not a matter of external but of internal thinking. No happiness is possible without action. It is only through action that all achievement is possible. No conceptualization can take you to Mount Everest. It is only your efforts to get there which will help you.

Don't Worry — Be Happy

Happiness is the best of all protection. It makes the invisible visible. It transforms the ordinary into something extraordinary. It also can also make the weak powerful. It can turn a fancy into a reality. It is the imagination which creates everything. It transforms ordinary people into heroes. It is a storehouse and a reservoir of power.

Happiness is power which can reduce a fire to ashes. Man is inherently neither good nor bad. His social usefulness and personal efficiency depend on his individual training, inclination and his personality. A person may sometimes not be aware of his individual strength and moral and creative capacities. All of us are capable of controlling our own actions. Emotions are not our masters. They are and should be used as tools.

You need to be motivated by convictions, attitudes and goals which you set for yourself. You can influence and change your own destiny. It is human nature to be aware more of what is done to us than what we do to others. The biggest and greatest obstacle to full development and co-operation with others is an underestimation of our own strength. Unfortunately, some environmental factors and approach to life tend to instil false concepts and attitudes about oneself in comparison with others. Our cultural patterns fortify them. The greatest enemy of mankind is fear. Courage and belief in our own ability are the basis of all achievement and virtues. The basis of all harmonious human relationships is the respect for your own dignity and respect for the rights and dignity of others. Settlement of conflicts through force or appeasement upsets the social equilibrium.

Every member of society is entitled to the same dignity and respect which all of us want for ourselves. Any assumption of superiority or inferiority on the basis of any incidental factors is not only arbitrary and fallacious but is also discriminatory and bad for self-esteem. The Bible says, "Do unto others as you would have others do unto you." All of us face discouraging and demoralizing experiences from time to time. We need to fortify ourselves with good intentions and support each other. The best and the most beautiful things in the world cannot be seen or even touched. They have to be felt with love. It is only through the heart that all inspiration comes. Learn to be full-hearted in dealing with yourself and dealing with others. Our best is expressed only through the heart. Deep emotions of joy and sorrow all come from the heart. Never sell your soul either for silver or gold. The soul residing in the heart is the best life insurance to keep us on the right track. Give the world your best. The best will come back to you. It is not possible to put a sign on the heart that it is not a thoroughfare. Time is a great healer of hurts, sorrows and disappointments. When one door closes, another door will open. It is only a question of keeping your eyes open and not losing heart. Never be satisfied with small things. Aim for the top. Do not be satisfied with the 'little and the less' in life. If you do so, you will become pygmies. Arise, awake and continue striving till you reach your goal. The greatest creation of God is man. There is nothing greater than the human mind. There is nothing greater than thought in the mind. In thought there is nothing greater than confidence and faith. You should spread

> Courage and belief in our own ability are the basis of all achievement and virtues.

joy and happiness and let no one leave you without feeling better and happier. No night of problems can defeat the sunrise of hope. Never be sharp in your speech as a sharp tongue sometimes cuts its own throat. The virtue of all achievement is the victory over one's weaknesses. Those who realize this will never know defeat.

Being right gives you immense confidence. Each new challenge should motivate you to further achievements and greater heights.

We should push ourselves as well as our motivation to bigger and better things. We need to start moving and know how much is 'too little and too much'. It is best to work to a deadline. It gets us going and keeps us going. However, to be useful it should be realistic. When you are used to doing little work you become resentful when more work comes your way. A simple minimalistic life is the best for most of us. Treat life as an easy drive on a smooth road.

What we want most is less of more to make our life comfortable and clutter free. Everyday is a time to purge the bulging closets, junk drawers, half-finished projects and cluttered bedrooms and drawing rooms which leave no living space. Our life is controlled by unnecessary goods which demand attention for repairs, filing, insuring and dry cleaning. Fewer choices leave you relatively freer and stress-free for achieving greater things in life. It is the old stuff you hold on to that keeps you from new possibilities or opportunities. You can start making your life simpler by throwing out 20 items per day.

It is true that getting rid of things collected over the years is not easy to do. You can justify retention and preservation of anything. But the more you throw away the more free you will feel. Most of us find hard to give up old books as if by holding onto them we will somehow acquire all their knowledge and wisdom. You can try throwing away a box full of half-finished projects and reports. This will definitely make you feel less cluttered. All of us constantly need to unclutter and free ourselves from long-held hurts, resentments and far too many regrets. There is a clutter not only of things which needs to be thrown away but also of the excess baggage of pre-conceived opinions and thoughts.

Almost all of us need to be motivated at one time or the other for forging ahead in life. This is the only way to combat and overcome failure. While some can be motivated by others there are others who can motivate themselves. People should discover which category they fall into. The latter category is a boon to an organization for they are high achievers and thus remain self-motivated. A success-oriented person is always willing to take personal responsibility for his actions. He wants credit for the success but is equally prepared to accept the blame for failure. He does not pass the buck. He prefers skills and competence over luck or chance. Such a person will not balance excessive odds against his ventures. He puts in that extra effort to achieve his goals. He persists in the

> It is only faith in ourselves and our hard work which can bring success.

face of adversity. His self-confidence does not allow him to be discouraged by failure. He never leaves a task unfinished. When the odds are very high he does not hesitate to change tactics. He is more goal-oriented than technique-oriented. For him the right method is the method which will give the best results and not necessarily an old tried one. He is creative, ingenious in adapting and modifying whatever is at hand to solve the problem. He is always scaling new heights of achievement. He is not satisfied with the status-quo nor with what he has achieved. As soon as he has attained one goal he sets his sight on a new goal. He is a self motivator with a positive attitude towards life. He is future-oriented but at the same time he addresses himself with maximum effort to the task of the moment. He perceives each current task, no matter how minor, as the most important job in itself.

Life is full of both sweet and sour experiences. If at times we are rewarded for our deeds, at others we are criticized. Almost everyone including the success-oriented person faces such situations in life. Both have equal importance in the development of personality, career and life. It is only faith in ourselves and our hard work which can bring success. The aim of all endeavour in life is to be a winner. The biggest challenge in life is life itself. Let us face the challenges and overcome despair. It is not difficult and a steely determination can meet all challenges and take us to the destination that we have decided on.

Bounce With Enthusiasm All The Time

Enthusiastic vibes are infectious irrespective of the source from where they come. Your enthusiasm will make your team brim with life and increase productivity. If you are enthusiastic, your team will reflect your mood. They will become enthusiastic themselves. A long face and a depressing demeanour can play havoc with group morale and affect the working of the entire organization. Good leaders always radiate good vibes so that their organization blossoms. Be optimistic about everything. If you see the bright side of things your subordinates also will look at the unfamiliar with enthusiasm and optimism. Optimism is generally a halfway house to a solution! Be passionate about your work and your job. This will have a positive effect on your people. Try to be a role model. Give a chance to others to emulate you.

Go Forward With A Smile

With the range of modern conveniences, appliances and gadgets and entertainment available one may be tempted to believe that man could keep his life action packed. However, a lot of people feel a void in their lives leading to disinterest and boredom. Depression and stress is no less in modern life despite all the gadgetry. Crimes like killing, rape, cheating and thefts continue at the same level. Craving for material things and getting rich quickly or acquiring material things immediately is still there. When people take short cuts and still do not get the desired results, disappointment follows. Quite often even after an individual has achieved one objective he is likely to take it for granted after sometime. The result is boredom and search for novelty to bring about a variety in life.

> Every individual
> is unique.

The solution to this problem is that each affected person should eliminate negative forces and have some interesting work. Boredom results quite often from not having enough to do. Another solution is to simplify your lifestyle. Take joy in little things like warm bonding in friendships and relationships. Recall happy memories with your family, friends and colleagues to feel positive and cheerful. Activities like going for a picnic, visiting friends and playing games regularly put you in a positive frame of mind. A few ground rules are essential for success and effective management. Firstly, respect the views, values, feelings and self-esteem of others. Every individual is entitled to be treated as a human being and with respect. Every individual is unique. He has been gifted by God with vastly different abilities to think, feel and seek self-fulfilment in his own way.

Whatever may be generally said in favour of arguing forcefully, it is a fact that an argument is likely to generate heated exchanges. It sometimes brings about conflicts and the worst in a human being. It is also true that without arguments you cannot present your case properly. Arguments based on facts and reasons and politely presented is the proper way to get your ideas and suggestion across.

Do not use arguments to release pent-up feelings, or to retaliate. Sometimes a casual remark is enough to put a person in a violent mood. This is particularly so when it is unjustified. Arguments drain energy and can lead to exhaustion. An argument can ruin any relationship. Arguments with self-opinionated and pompous people are best avoided. Nobody is a winner in any argument. The person who loses an argument is unhappy. The winner instead of securing a friend would probably add an enemy to his list. Therefore, argue in such a manner so that the other person does not feel that he is being coerced to agree to your logic. For a winner it is essential to remember that a bad mood is always the result of a negative or depressing thought. The only remedy for bad moods is to cancel their effect by creating cheering and uplifting thoughts. Moods are very fragile and unpredictable commodities but you can always change them by pleasing and appreciating yourself. Gather your courage and energy to be in a good mood. Try to concentrate on the things which cheer you up and at all costs do not listen to flatterers who are usually in subordinate or lower positions than you. It may cost you your success and happiness. Always have high expectations from yourself. Such expectations are the secret of all achievement.

Many times you will face situations in life which are depressing. You may also feel that it is the end of your world. At that time remember the following poem of Rudyard Kipling:

If you can keep your head when all about you
Are losing theirs and blaming it on you;
If you can trust yourself when all men doubt you
But make allowances for their doubting too;
If you can wait and not be tired by waiting;
Or being lied about, don't deal in lies
Or being hated, don't give way to hating
And yet don't look too good nor talk too wise;
If you can dream — and not make dreams your master;
If you can think — and not make thoughts your aim;
If you can meet with triumph and disaster
And treat those two impostors just the same;
If you can hear the truth you've spoken
Twisted by knaves to make a trap for fools;
Or watch the things you gave your life to broke
And stoop and build me up with worn-out tools;
If you can make one heap of all your winnings

And risk it on one turn of pitch and toss
And lose and start again at your beginnings
And never breathe a word about your loss;
If you can force your heart and nerve and sinew
To serve your turn long after they are gone;
And so hold on when there is nothing in you
Except the will which says to them, 'Hold on';
If you can talk with crowds and keep your virtue
Or walk with kings — nor lose the common touch;
If neither foes nor loving friends can hurt you;
If all men count with you but none too much;
If you can fill the unforgiving minute
With sixty seconds worth of distance run
Yours is the Earth and everything that's in it
And which is more — you'll be a Man my Son.

It is essential to remember that success and failure are the two sides of the same coin. You have no control over circumstances but you have control over your own attitude in a given set of circumstances. This should help you determine your attitude towards a particular situation. Every adverse situation is bound to pass away. Every achievement is largely the outcome of steadily raising one's level of aspiration and expectations. Each one of us is given a fixed amount of time to spend. It is up to us to use it well. We can make the best use of it or waste it. Also, we can never get a day back whatever price we may be willing to pay.

> ★ We have to accept that being imperfect is part of the human condition.

Absolute perfection exists in fiction. We need not strain ourselves for attaining perfection to impress others. God loves us the way we are in all our conditions. Our effort should be to become the best we can be. We have to accept that being imperfect is part of the human condition. We strive to be complete when we are imperfect. People around us, our parents, our colleagues want us to be flawless or at least steadily show improvement in our conduct and achievements. Any reaction or emotion should be attributed to a deed and not to a person. Never encourage an emotion which paralyzes you with a sense of unworthiness and destructiveness. By doing something wrong we start a war between the good part of our personality and the part which has done something unworthy or is contemplating to do so.

We must learn to come to terms with our limitations. Life does not guarantee success to the best all the time. It is neither a kind of a game where one mistake disqualifies you for life. It is a game where even the worst have a chance to show their brilliance. It is an enterprise where efforts should be directed towards winning more often than abandoning effort and losing. Never be afraid of competition. It fosters and improves the quality of goods and services.

Maintaining motivation at a high level is difficult. One has to make a constant effort not to give way to depression and temporary setbacks. In fact a setback should be looked upon as a temporary phase and not a permanent trauma. Consistency and constancy are essential in keeping the light of motivation burning. This is the only way to achieve success in any field of life. It has been correctly observed that "Genius is ninety percent perspiration and ten percent inspiration."

One way to success is to set achievable goals within a given time span. Attaining of small well-defined goals will go a long way in convincing yourself that you have a potential for success and you are capable of greater achievements. Even if you have some big goals to achieve divide them into smaller manageable sub-goals and target them. You will suddenly realize that by putting them together the larger picture becomes clearer. Model yourself on the pattern of the successful person you admire most. Have your heroes. It is difficult, if not impossible, to pattern your success in accordance with an abstract ideal. It is best to base it on a living ideal or objective. This will motivate you to success on a continuous basis. Somerset Maugham has remarked, "The common idea that success spoils people by making them vain, egoistic and self-complacent is erroneous. On the contrary it makes them for the most part humble, tolerant and kind." Anatole de Laforge writes, "The objective of any performance is success. All the virtues and the joys are contained in one word 'Success'. Success is a fulfilment."

You have to learn to manage stress in your own way so that you can perform brilliantly. One way you can cope with stress is to leave your work behind when you leave your workplace. Maintaining good health should be as important as your doing your job well. You can expect more from yourself and your career only if you are fit to work. Only then will your performance be in tune with your competence. Peter Drucker remarks: "To be a good manager is something but to be an effective manager is much more." It is strange but true though not always so that all good people

★ **Nobody is perfect.**

are not clever and all clever people are not good. It would be a better world than we imagine if the above combination was to exist in a vast majority of people. The essential of good governance is to create a climate where new skills can be acquired easily and meaningfully. It is equally essential to provide facilities, a work climate and a work culture for good governance. No order, directive or plan can bring about a change unless the persons directly affected and charged with the responsibility of bringing about the change absorb the meaning of it and are committed to implementing it. To get the best out of the people working for you it is essential to make it clear to them from the beginning as to what is expected of them. Nobody is perfect. You have to guide people and help them in improving their performance. Humiliating others does not improve matters and does not pay in the long run. But at the same time the implications of infraction of discipline should be clearly explained to them so that they know well in advance the resultant consequences. Black is black and white is white. They remain so both during darkness and daylight. Personal values and ethics which are the sum total of moral conduct are important for everybody. It is not possible for man to avoid action as worldly life involves action. The Gita says, "Man does not attain freedom from action without entering upon action; nor does he reach perfection merely by ceasing to act. None can remain inactive even for a moment for everyone is helplessly

"Speak softly and carry a big stick and you will go far", advised Roosevelt.

driven to action by nature. Therefore, do your allotted duty for action, it is superior to inaction." Duties can differ according to the station of one's birth and conditions in life. While working remember to have profound respect for your work and be totally indifferent to the results. Always work to the best of your ability.

"Speak softly and carry a big stick and you will go far," advised Roosevelt. Discipline is essential in life for solving myriads of problems. Procrastinating or ignoring problems does not help. They have to be solved immediately to prevent future headaches. You have to assume responsibility for your own life. The only way to success is to make ceaseless efforts for achieving your goals and face deprivations and privations, if necessary. First, complete the task assigned to you before you sit back and enjoy life. Children coming from school have to do their homework before they can go out to play. The pleasure of games and other fun must be postponed until the homework is done. The same is true in life. Delaying personal relaxation or pleasure till the work required to be done is done is the basic rule to success. This approach will give you tremendous peace of mind. To improve the employees in your organization you must give performance pep-talk to poor performers and motivate them to do better.

Managers should distinguish between high performers and low achievers. It has to be kept in mind that nobody can or will learn new and better methods of performance unless there is motivation. People should be motivated to realize that additional knowledge or skills will help them in bettering their performance and achievement. It is a fact that new arrivals in an organization and those experimenting with new ideas will readily agree to try new methods than others who might have been on the scene for a longer time. Some of the senior workers will think that they know more than others. It has to be repeatedly dinned into them that the winds of change are not always harmful.

Ways To Beat A Bad Mood

Due to hectic lifestyles and pressures that most people face everyday it is not surprising that they experience bad moods. Being in a bad mood can seriously interfere with our work, relationships with colleagues, superiors, subordinates as well as home life. It is generally noticed in several studies that women are almost twice likely to suffer from bad moods and depression as compared to men. It is because women spend a lot more time thinking about what is making them unhappy. This brooding sometimes over trifles can lead to bad moods. Whenever you are feeling low, do not wallow in self-pity. Instead take action to shed off that oppressive feeling. By behaving and thinking cheerfully you will feel better immediately.

1. Change your thinking for the better

Generally, we are what and how we think. Negative thinking is black and will generate a black mood. Each one of us can have a full command over our thoughts. The only condition is that you should gain control of your mind and become aware of the bleak thinking and negative patterns that induce a negative frame of mind. After becoming aware of negative thoughts replace them with positive and good thoughts. With practice you can and will break the depressing, negative and vicious circle. Optimistic thoughts will produce a corresponding mood of hope and enthusiasm.

2. Socialization is a good cure for bad moods

A person in a bad mood does not like being around happy people. It is important to note that if you isolate yourself you will only focus on your misery and what is causing you to feel low. If you are ever in such a condition, invite a friend, call on him or meet for a meal and divert your mind by chatting. A change of scene, atmosphere and company will have an uplifting and positive effect on your mood.

3. Be active in defeating bad moods

Any delay in facing an unpleasant task which is hanging over your head will only put you in a bad mood. Delayed action in dealing with any unpleasant situation only prolongs your agony. You should save yourself the pain by tackling difficulties and problems as they arise. It may be making a phone call, firing somebody, conveying bad news or anything which you have been dreading doing. Brace yourself for it and tackle it headlong. It will make you feel much better.

4. Mix only with positive persons

Having happy and positive people around is a great way to cheer yourself up. It will take your mind off your problems. Share your feelings and the reasons why you are feeling what you are feeling. Misery shared is misery halved. Associate with positive persons to talk about your problems and seek their guidance. It will lift up your spirits.

5. Prioritizing and delegating is another way to beat bad moods

Being overwhelmed with work or responsibilities at home can

also lead to bad moods. Prioritizing and delegating work can help in overcoming distress. Number your daily tasks from ten to one, one being the most important task and the others in descending order of importance. If possible, delegate the less important ones or take the help of others for doing them. Getting over the most important tasks will cheer you up. Never feel ashamed in asking for help.

6. Be helpful

Helping those who are less fortunate than you will make you realize that your own problems are rather insignificant as compared to the misfortunes of some other persons. Visit an ailing relative, help a friend and do some volunteer work with a charity organization to appreciate how fortunate you are in your life.

7. Avoid the blame game

Whenever a misfortune occurs, do not blame others for it. If you do so, you will continue to remain powerless and will not be able to change how you feel by blaming others. Accept responsibility for your actions. Take control of the situation to uplift your mood. Be in charge of your own life yourself. Feeling happy, cheerful and good is your own responsibility and not of others.

8. Cut out the negativity

Your outlook on life, your mood and your life will be the first to suffer if you continuously bombard yourself with the thoughts that you are hopeless and a failure. The moment you do away with the self-critical self-talk your mood will begin to lift. Talk back to yourself when your inner voice tells you that you are a failure and not good enough. Tell it that you are a winner and not a loser. Tell it that you totally disagree with any depressing thoughts

9. Focus on the present

Bad moods are the result of wallowing in the past or worrying about what is going to happen in the future. It has no basis in reality. It only shows that you are avoiding the present. Find a solution to your present problem. Day-dreaming or escaping from the present is passive. Nobody in this world has found the answers to his problems by staring at the wall or brooding all by himself.

10. Be novel by trying something totally new

Bad moods can also be due to being stuck in a rut or in negative grooves. You should try involving yourself in a new hobby, social work or anything which enthuses you. Embarking on a new activity will divert your mind and produce a good mood as a side-effect. You can try any new activity like yoga, running, singing very loudly, or dancing. Make an effort to be on a natural high all the time. Chase away your negative state of mind which can lead to a loss of interest in life, health problems like insomnia, fatigue and other incidental problems. Do not hesitate to consult your doctor for any signs of depression. Never think twice before deciding to seek professional help if you cannot handle anything on your own.

Choose The Right Approach

Stress can result from conflict or financial loss, an unfortunate love affair or anything unpleasant or tragic. It is our body and mind which react to various situations and produce stress. Perverse thoughts, unpleasant bodily sensations, feelings, emotions and odd behaviour are the results of stress. During stress a trifling remark is magnified and a normal gesture is misunderstood. Negative apprehensions add to our misery and lead to increased stress. Stress can affect the body and cause tension in the limbs, pain in the head and neck, pressure in the chest, an upset stomach, inability to sleep and a mental breakdown. We need to recognize and rationalize our psychological feelings and emotions during stress. Under stress we get angry, agitated, anxious, depressed or suspicious. These negative emotions multiply and add to stress.

It is important to be self-conscious of our own behaviour and conduct towards and during stress. We should choose healthy ways of coping with it instead of skipping our physical exercise, smoking or drinking excessively, driving recklessly and being short tempered with everyone over whom we have control. These only add to the problems of ill-health. They will start another unending vicious cycle of stress. Dealing with stress requires us to take into consideration our thoughts, bodily sensations, emotions and behaviour. If

> Dwelling on negative thoughts only adds to stress.

you can control them, you can control stress The first important factor is to recognize as to what is happening at various levels. Only then steps can be taken to do away with factors which cause stress. This will reverse the process steadily but surely. The negative habit of brooding and worrying when things do not go our way does not help anybody.

We must learn to tackle stress at the thought level. A chain of depressing thoughts is the source of stress. In a conflict at office with colleagues or a fight with your wife, begin by asking yourself whether the fight was worth it. Also, ask yourself as to how it is going to contribute to your success and welfare in your life. If it is not something earth-shaking, then stop thinking about it. If it is important, find out less stressful ways of accomplishing your goals. Go ahead and take action but do not brood. It is also important to take charge of your mind at all times. One way is to divert it and get busy with something more absorbing or more interesting. Dwelling on negative thoughts only adds to stress.

Every individual responds to stress in a different way as each one of us is unique. Stress gives headaches to some while some others have an upset stomach, difficulty in breathing or start crying, over-eating, yelling or losing temper over trifles. It is important to recognize your own pattern so that you can be prepared to deal with it. Knowing your own symptoms of stress works like a personal thermometer of stress. Knowing the problem and its solution is the first step in mastering it. It is up to each one of us to deal with stress in our own style whether it is through sports, yoga, meditation or entertainment. Stress by its very compulsion will generate negative emotions such as anger, irritability, anxiety, hopelessness, depression etc. The best course is to recognize your feelings and the factors which generate it. Stress has no rationale. It manifests as a reaction to an unwelcome environment, persons or events. A quarrel in the office or home can leave you irritable. The irritation can express itself in a fight with children, your wife or your colleagues. A positive emotion replacing a negative one is the only way to overcome stress. Relaxation and listening to your favourite music or watching your favourite TV programme, listening to the radio and visiting friends are other ways of reducing stress. Being helpful and altruistic gives a happy and positive feeling of self-worth and confidence.

It is easy to be negative during a period of stress and fall prey to habits of excessive smoking, drinking, over-eating or consuming sedatives. These are pernicious habits which lead only to a one way journey downhill. They are not a permanent solution to the problem of stress. Long-term solutions are cultivation of good company, friends, socializing, immersing yourself in work, taking exercise and giving your best to the organization for which you are working. It is just not possible to prevent stressful life events. Crises dog everyone's life. We can and should prepare and train ourselves in such a way that whenever a stressful event occurs in our life and we have to confront it we should be able to manage it in a satisfactory way. Coping with stress is also a day-to-day affair. The long-term measures include developing a healthy lifestyle and organizing your life from the early years in a disciplined and balanced way with time for both work, play, sleep and interpersonal relationships. Excessive smoking or drinking should be avoided and developing spiritual values in life will go a long way to make life stable, sane and secure. Life has a greater purpose than only eating, drinking, working and making money. The greater purpose to life is giving your best to society and with a stress-free life the speed of accomplishment is not only better but also greater.

Stress Busters

Every person has problems which can lead to stress. Many get bogged down and do not know how to deal with stress. Here are some suggestions and observations which may help:

1. Every event in life, however adverse, has a plus side. It is just a question of looking closely as well as tracing and spotting the advantage.

2. Do not feel sorry or remorseful about any mistakes made in the past. The past is dead and gone. It is no more than a ghost. Do not worry about the future. It is still to come. The most important thing is the present. Make it positive, creative and joyful.

3. Never compare yourself with others. You are unique in your own way.

4. Do not be jealous of others. It is a waste of time and energy. It neither helps you nor harms the person of whom you are jealous.

5. Every person has some qualities which are superior to others. Others may be superior to you in some ways as you would no doubt be to others in some other ways.

6. Do not fritter away your time and energy in trying to solve several problems at the same time. Open only one front

at a time to decimate the problem. Put maximum efforts to solve one problem at a time before you tackle the next.

7. If a problem does not get solved immediately, despite all efforts, do not be too unhappy. Time, the best healer, will solve it or may provide even a better solution.

8. Your critics are your best friends and well-wishers. They point out your weaknesses. It is best to examine the points raised by them. Do not indulge in backbiting. A gentleman does not backbite.

9. Revenge is both negative and debilitating. It is best to try to forgive and forget.

10. Surrender all your worries and problems to God. He will guide you to the right solution.

11. Observe yourself for any defeatist or negative thoughts. Fill your mind with good thoughts of health, happiness and confidence to counter any negativity.

12. Laughter is the best antidote to stress. Laugh at yourself when you make mistakes. Develop a capacity to make fun of your own idiosyncrasies. Do not laugh at the predicament of others.

13. Meditation, contemplation and thinking peaceful thoughts will bring peace, poise and relaxation of the mind and body. It will enable you to do your best.

14. Be realistic in setting your goals. Increase the range and productivity of your goals as you move along the highway of success.

15. Turn grudges into a sustenance for life. Rather than being simply an expression of vindictiveness, grudges should remind you to how to bring order and behave in a becoming manner in your own life. Be personally accountable to yourself for all your actions. Bitterness and resentment only add to the misery if you go on brooding as to how to harm others for the hurt that they have caused you. This attitude of feeling wronged all the time will spoil your relationships for a long time to come. If you have a strong sense of right and wrong, of what is just and unjust, a grudge will drag you down until what has caused it ends. Be prepared to do something about the grudge to end it soon. Never be afraid of confronting the person and the cause of the grudge. Simmering and suffering in silence is like a slow poisoning. We should not be uncomfortable with the idea that any behaviour is unforgivable. We should move on and let bygones be bygones. A grudge can kill you. Those who harbour hostile thoughts have a higher risk of dying of heart disease. Narrow-mindedness, maliciousness and vengefulness are deadly emotions to be avoided.

Turn your anger and resentment into something constructive and positive. Do not carry this heavy baggage all the time. You should express your displeasure by a direct statement rather than by an emotional outburst. You do not always have to hold a grudge or harbour resentment over every action of others. Let the person who has hurt you know that you are hurt. It will lessen the chances of it being repeated later on. Communicate effectively what you feel. Communication is the art of conveying clearly so that the other person understands exactly in the way you want him to understand.

The purpose of communication is to satisfy our needs, establish relationships, create understanding between ourselves and others as well as cause changes and share experiences, frustrations, hopes and fears.

Communication is vital for the development and maintenance of relationships. Others cannot read our minds. It is for us to let them know about our wishes and expectations. The ability to communicate effectively is acquired like any other skill. Life is competitive. Success usually comes to those who are prepared to make extra efforts to acquire this skill. The right attitude is another important factor in effective communication. Clarity in communication is vital. Ambiguity leads to pressure, stress, errors and costly mistakes. To be clear in your thinking is to be efficient. Communication enables us to stay in touch with the world around us.

Every employee from the lowest echelon upwards looks up to the top man for guidance and leadership. The top man sets the tone for the development of personality, health and direction of the organization. This is evident at every level of behaviour in the organization.

> The leader has to earn respect by leading from the front.

The real challenge before the leader is how to build and motivate a team so that it is able to perform at optimum efficiency. The leader's personality, goals, his qualities of being an open, encouraging and frank boss who keeps all channels of discussion open and transparent can transform the organization's culture to strive for excellence at every opportunity. Like people organizations, too, have a personality.

Persons working there need to have a sense of identification and commitment to it. The role of the leader is to make it happen. The employees should feel that their leader is the person who will take them and the organization to new heights. It is said about Bill Gates and his company Microsoft that it is led by a genius who also has the foresight to recognize the genius in others. The top man is the organization's number one brand manager as well as an ambassador. All his actions one way or the other will impact the way it is perceived and recognized. In the new global economy organizations will be so structured that its members function as a team of wealth generators in letter and spirit especially when the rate of obsolescence coupled with global competition is fairly high. It is up to the top man to take charge and adapt his enterprise to the prevailing conditions.

Leadership is also about charisma. The leader has to earn respect by leading from the front. Occasionally, the system has to be fine-tuned. The pendulum can swing from one extreme to the other depending upon the type of boss. Perhaps a mixture of an authoritative and participatory environment can be the best approach and combination. Effective and stress-free functioning is all about striking equilibrium between short and long-term strategies.

Uncluttering the mind is more important than removing physical clutter. It will also make you more efficient and productive. It will also help you understand as to who can be depended upon to deliver the goods. The effort should be not only to unclutter your physical surroundings but also mental cobwebs. Uncluttering requires not only will-power but also some ruthlessness. However, any action and planning in this direction does not guarantee that you will have a problem-free life. If God gives any problem, be sure that He will also give you the strength to face it. Do not magnify problems. It is the fate of man to suffer gain and loss, to laugh and shed tears, to be periodically happy and unhappy. You have to make a conscious effort to train your mind to look at the positive aspect of everything that happens to you.

7

RESOURCES TO
REINVENT YOURSELF

It Is Up To You

Your values in life are the cornerstone of your character. It is
only by living by your values that you fulfil yourself. Values get
reflected in your work and performance as well as your lifestyle.
You can rise in life by living your values. It is your values which
hold you back or give a push to your success in life. Values
create a vision and a desire for excellence. Living and working
by one's values is sometimes difficult, but it is more rewarding
than any other temporary success.

Everything in life needs management. More than any other
management, time management is most
important. If you can manage time
properly you can have time for
everything you want to do. It requires
adjustment but this is the only way you

> ★ Attitude is as
> important as
> skills.

can fulfil your ambitions in life. The explosion in knowledge and information in the present times is overwhelming. For success, each one of us has to keep pace with the latest developments. Knowledge is not something static. It has to be replenished and renewed periodically to keep pace with the changing times. If it is not renewed or updated, it becomes a product which has outlived its life. Our economy, our lives, our jobs and professions are knowledge driven. Always give enough time to yourself to regroup and plan your ideas and put them into action. Take time to renew yourself. If you look around, you will notice plenty of opportunities. Success is simply encashing the opportunities which keep on knocking at our doors for attention.

Develop the knack of getting your due from others. Attitude is as important as skills. Sometimes a positive attitude can compensate for any skill. The ingredients of your attitude should always be appropriateness and correctness. It should have the approval of both your head and heart. Set your goals after careful deliberation. Having done so you should go all out to achieve them. Keeping yourself on your pre-determined path and focused on your objective can alone lead you to success. Never have a closed mind or preconceived notions about any approach, method or persons for achieving your success. Always keep on building your intellectual capital. You should always make that extra effort to stay ahead. High standards are only one element in the recipe for success. They should be revised once you have achieved one set of goals. Guard yourself against obsolence. New discoveries, inventions and technology can easily and very quickly make the present-day approaches and methods obsolete. Keep up with changing times and find ways of using new inventions and discoveries as well as the technology of tomorrow. Your success depends on how quickly you can use them. A few decades ago everybody believed that television was only meant for entertainment. Now it is taken as a vehicle for social and attitudinal changes. The internet and e-mail were foreign words a few years ago. A fax machine was a rarity and it was only the telex or a teleprinter which was regarded as the latest technology in transmitting the written word. The very idea of mobile or cellular phones was considered as something only for the gods but today it has become a reality. It depends upon each one of us to put to best use the discoveries and inventions not only for the betterment of the society but also for our own progress and moving ahead in life. An American poet Ella Wheeler Wilcox says:

One ship drives east and another drives west
With the selfsame winds that blow.
This the set of sails and not gales
Which tells us the way to go!

We always learn from our own and others' experiences as well as mistakes. One way to have fun in one's job is to separate a problem from other activities and then concentrate on the problem to find out its solution. Attempting a solution itself leads to a number of activities. The final outcome of all such activities is the solving of the problem. All initiatives start and end with a person attempting to solve any problems or difficulties. It is for us to clarify our doubts about any

> It is up to each one of us to be our best friend or our worst enemy.

problems by either checking up with our friends or colleagues, experts or the information available on the internet. We should learn to personalize our knowledge to keep ourselves on the top. We should cultivate dreams that will outlive us. We should take up challenges with a firm belief in ourselves. God has empowered each one of us with inner courage and resources. He has given us energy to achieve excellence in our chosen fields. It is up to each one of us to be our best friend or our worst enemy. It is again up to each one of us to either indulge in or cut out the blame game. It is easy to find alibis or a blameworthy object to explain away or account for our own failures. The alibi for failure can be in the form of a person, an event or a place. The responsibility for our success or failure is our own. It is up to each one of us to build self-confidence in ourselves. Our effort should be to charter our life towards consistent and positive improvement and achievement of new goals. Be on the fast track. Make it a habit to have an exhilarating journey through life. There is always a link between your learning, knowledge and skills and your livelihood in life. No situations are similar. Still other people's experience can sometimes point out the right direction instead of discovering it through making mistakes.

Success in life is all about the attitudes we cultivate and display in our lives. What you get in life is in direct proportion to your attitude. It is strange but true that each one of us contributes in making our attitude what it is. There is nothing wrong in being ambitious as long as one puts one's heart and soul to achieve clear objectives and goals. Never be impatient and over-demanding when looking for immediate results. You have to learn to be fair and ethical both to the people you work for and work with. Potential can be developed to the maximum if you develop your self-confidence and tackle intelligently any problem that comes your way. Punctuality in the performance of your work should not be periodical and sporadic. It is something which should become a habit and a convenience. If you can keep your house spick and span remember to keep your office or workplace also in the same condition. Make it a point to keep your office a model of your well-kept house. It should be an extension of your house.

There is no justification to keep your workplace cluttered where you spend one third of your life. If you resent thick dust on various items in your house, your office items should be treated in the same way. The extended lunch breaks, the long gossip sessions treating the office as a place for socialization are not conductive to success. Long brooding or resentment session over office orders are not the means or methods to reach the top. Time should be spent on upgrading your skills. There are no rewards for unskilled people. Do not be under the illusion that the world owes you a living. It should be your priority to solve problems and not seek or give justification as to why things have not been done well. Find time to take up new responsibilities so that you get the reputation of a person who looks to the future with intelligence and vision. Intellectual obsolescence has no rewards anywhere in the world. If you do not change and improve with the times you will not only remain underemployed or unemployed but you may become unemployable. You should remove stones and obstacles of inefficiency from the path of your work and organization. Never give excuses when things go wrong or try to win points when the performance is on a downhill path. Do not expect your organization to take care of your expectations unless you first take care of it. Do not turn the definition of punctuality topsy-turvy by coming late and going away early. It reflects a callous and inefficient attitude towards everything. Decide where you want to reach and you will. Cash in on the opportunities that come your way. A poet said:

> *There was a very cautious man*
> *Who never laughed or played*
> *He never risked, he never tried,*
> *He never sang or prayed;*
> *And when he one day passed away*
> *His insurance was denied*
> *For since he never really lived*
> *They claimed he never died.*

The choice is entirely up to each one of us to become what we wish to become.

The Winner Takes All

People who believe that they will succeed whether realistically or not are more likely to succeed. They elicit respect and attention. They present a posture of confidence and success which proclaims to the world that they will succeed. Hence, they win the respect and attention of others.

Self-confidence is more powerful than will-power. Most of the time we behave in accordance with what we think of ourselves. Our brains have stored a great deal of information about

> ★ Our thoughts take us in the desired direction.

ourselves like the kind of person we are, our skills, our abilities, our appearance and our competence. We respond to any emergency or a normal situation in accordance with the information in our data-bank. A belief in our competence leads us to accept challenges while a person who thinks he is incapable will find excuses to avoid challenges. Self-confidence coupled with an intense desire to achieve a goal almost guarantees success. A desire fuelled with passion accelerates the process. Our thoughts take us in the desired direction. They push our actions forwards and goad them to achieve our dreams. Positive thinking without a smouldering desire to achieve a goal is not sufficient.

Our feelings and thoughts are complementary. They arise from each other. Our thought and emotional systems do not know the difference between reality and dreams. They believe whatever is fed to them. Even in the safety of our homes a horror movie evokes a kind of feeling as if we are in danger. The fate of a hero or a heroine makes many people cry when watching a film as if they were playing the film role. Our adrenal glands pump adrenaline into our bloodstream leading to pleasant or unpleasant reactions depending upon the scenario being presented or seen.

A comfortless existence, a verbal fight with anybody in the morning could still leave us angry till night. We play all such incidents in our imagination like a stuck needle on a record. The body keeps on releasing adrenaline into our system because of the continued imaginary fights in our mind. We go on re-enacting the stressful events of the past. It does not end there. Many people continue anticipating next day's problems and stresses. This is what keeps most people in a state of perpetual stress. Over a period of time these thoughts start telling on the body to the point of exhaustion and a nervous breakdown. People do not realize that resentments and hatred hurt them more than the individuals at whom they are directed. Misery, imaginary happenings and anticipating the worst rather than the best can make healthy individuals sick. Being angry, unhappy and depressed will raise your blood pressure leading to possible chronic blood pressure and heart problems. This approach and lifestyle will lead to a weakening of emotions and the immune system. People in poor health suffering from incurable diseases but with a positive attitude and belief that their health is good have a higher chance of survival and a happier life than those in good health who believe that their health is poor. Pessimism and a fossilized approach to life are the major causes of problems in life.

Optimistic, cheerful and positive thinkers expect to solve their problems and get well in a hurry. They also give themselves the most compelling reason that they cannot afford the luxury of being out of the race to succeed. Hence, they get well quickly. They also have something to live for. This attitude promotes rapid healing in case such people fall sick. Rapid healers are found to have something to look forward to not only for living but also for their goals.

Using your mental faculties makes you creative and gives you more life force. Creative workers like writers, scientists, inventors, painters, philosophers, and inventors not only live longer but remain productive longer than non-creative workers.

> ★ It might take a little time but the most important thing is to make a beginning.

An enthusiasm for life will create a need for more life. It in turn will make your living purposeful, full of verve and energy. It will generate a cycle of more life. Faith, courage, interest, optimism, looking forward to the times to come with expectation of something good happening will generate new life. Our thoughts are the greatest factors in our lives not only for today but also for tomorrow and the day after tomorrow. What we think today will determine our tomorrow.

We should not become slaves to a mindset or a frozen time frame situation. Unfortunately, it exists in a large measure both in managers and their men, their attitudes as well as products and the services rendered in our country. The type of products produced in our industries and their quality is the same day after day. No change for the better is possible by the rules and regulations framed in the nineteenth century which govern our economic and civic life even today. We are doing the same things over and over again but expecting different results.

It is for the managers and leaders to initiate changes and everybody will adjust to them. It might take a little time but the most important thing is to make a beginning. A thousand mile journey begins with the first step. For progress there is a need from time to time for a total transformation in the organizational culture. However, even small but continuous changes in all areas of our life can add value to our activities. To a great extent the responsibility for this lies in the approach and attitude of the top management. It is they and they alone who have the power, authority as well as the responsibility of promoting change and progress in their organization.

In the internet era when organizations are passing through

a major transition phase there is always an urgent need for a substantial amount of communication to be done with employees at different levels. As the level of specialization is escalating there is a requirement for faster and better flow of communication suitable to the needs of each employee. There is always both a cultural lag and competence level of different employees. One is not an exact copy of the other. Everywhere there is a requirement of specialists who can mobilize and direct employees to assimilate the information glut and convert it into knowledge-based solutions for advancement and progress of their organizations.

However, a specialist has to first acquire a thorough understanding of the work environment, work ethics and attitudes of the employees of the organization. He also has to be on a constant search for the latest information and channel it to the relevant levels for optimum results. His constant concern efforts and strategies should be to encourage a drive for continuous up-gradation of skills, knowledge and performance. The effort should be to tune in to the latest developments in IT and other areas in a way that contributes to the efficiency of your organization as well as by absorbing successful experiences of others. This requires keeping abreast with the latest technology breakthroughs all over the world and sharing new ideas and concepts with the people in your organization to improve their information processing ability. It also presupposes a nose for new events, new phenomena and happenings all around locally, nationally and globally. It also assumes that leaders will be able to foresee the extent to which any achievement would be possible in the light of available resources. It should almost be a self-imposed obligation to enjoy working and developing a team which believes in encouraging, fostering and excelling itself. There are bound to be unforeseen situations and changes in any organization or a situation. It is best to be flexible than rock the boat all the time. The effort should be to have a manpower fired with a quest for knowledge as well as competence committed to the organization with a clear sense of purpose.

There will always be scope as well as the need to work harder at achieving still higher goals in any organization. The trick lies in redefining your attitudes and making yourself more information-hungry. This will create an environment conducive to still higher learning and better performance.

Put Your Best Foot Forward

You should always be your genuine self and not a phoney. Never be self-opinionated and argumentative. Everybody avoids argumentative and conceited individuals. Always wear a cheerful smile on your face. Try to reach out to other people more than halfway or all the way necessary. Always remember that you are to nurture your relationships as you nurture a plant. A small incident can wreck a relationship as a small gesture can repair it. Basically everybody should realize the importance of cordial relationships not only with subordinates but also with equals. Many a time a problem arises as to who should take the first step in breaking the ice.

The personality of a person has two parts. One is character. It is invisible. The other is your external appearance, the manner of your conversation, the expression on your face and in the eyes. With charming and interesting conversation you can enchant people and sell yourself. It is a natural human tendency to look at successful people in their triumphant glory. The most important point of looking at these people is to find out how they reached where they are and what methods they adopted to reach the top. It is important to learn from their methods of working and organizational capabilities. Earnestness, sincerity of purpose and self discipline are the first steps towards putting your best foot forward.

Interest yourself in other people. Speak with life and emphasis in your daily conversation as well as when you address any formal meeting or a programme. Do not speak like a listless person. Dress the part you are playing at any given time. Be agreeable and pleasant at all times. Develop a regular habit of directing your attention to the most important facets of the job at hand. Distinguish between facts, rumours and information. Use whatever may be relevant to the occasion. Adopt a standard which should guide you in your conduct and work. You have absolute control to think the way you want to think. The only condition is that you must want to think in a particular way. There is a famous poem by Henley as under:

> *Out of the night that covers me*
> *Black as the pit from pole to pole*
> *I thank whatever gods may be*
> *For my unconquerable soul.*
> *In the full clutch of circumstances*
> *I have not winced or cried aloud.*
> *Under the bludgeoning of chance*
> *My head is bloody but unbowed.*

Beyond this place of wrath and tears
Looms but the horror of the shade
And yet the menace of the years
Finds and shall find me unafraid.

Sometimes one lands in a job or a place where there is not enough work for everybody. Everybody in such an organization wants a high profile job. In such circumstances trivial incidents become important. This leads to the start of vendettas and backbiting which are problems characteristic of overcrowded organizations. It is only in smaller units that people do not have time for trivia. Some unpopular slots are created to keep people who have fallen out of favour there. I myself have been posted to many such places during my thirty-six and half years of career in the Indian Police Service. But I never wasted my time. I was posted as a Deputy Inspector General of Police in-charge of the proposed State Industrial Security Force in Bangalore, Karnataka in 1984 and again in 1987. The Act had been passed by the State Assembly. But the rules had not been notified. The job given to me was a closed shop. I had no staff, no personal assistant and only one file. I decided to chart my way. I addressed all the Chief Executives of the Karnataka Government informing them that I had been given the responsibility of ensuring proper security to all the Government owned industries of the State Government and that I would be visiting their organizations to check their existing set-up and see how it could be improved without increasing the cost. The idea when translated into action was not only

> Build the reputation of a person who looks objectively at his failures and overcomes them.

appreciated but generated enough work to keep me happy. I had focused on the issue of doing my job properly however insignificant it was considered to be. I did not feel irritated at being dumped in a job in which I could not bask in its reflected glory. I made a success of it. I did not feel rancour at what many others perceived as unfair treatment. I had in my mind to maintain the long-term relationships with my self-esteem. Many of my sympathizers classified the job as a crash and a come down. They suggested that I seek the helpline of the politicians for a better placement. Some of them offered to help. My polite reply was that the pasture on the other side always looks greener under all circumstances. I would do my best. I learned more about the job which helped me enormously in dealing and working with different people.

The quality of decision-making can only transform your organization. An effective and no-nonsense leader has to realize that it does not matter who takes the first step. The most important factor in any job is the result. Only teamwork and co-ordination can contribute towards the overall performance. A leader should be a capable shock-absorber. Occasionally, he will have to take flak in the interest of the team and its larger interests. If you have made a mistake do not always harp on it. Put it behind you. You can review your mistakes. Critically review them only with the objective of not repeating them. Try to gain new insights related to the problems at hand. We all can always learn from our failures. But failure should not be a goal. Failure should teach only one lesson that it is the last thing wanted in life by anybody. Study your failures and obstacles only with a view to overcoming them. Build the reputation of a person who looks objectively at his failures and overcomes them.

Decide what is most important for your long-term, short-term and immediate plans. Try to live life in such a way that you make a habit of doing first things first. As a person aiming to give momentum to whatever you do, whether it be a proposal or a plan, shake yourself out of inertia and start implementing your plan.

If you are a top man, cut down the levels of decision-making to the minimum acceptable level so that efficiency is not hampered. It is ideal if the maximum levels for decision-making are limited to two. Anything more than three levels will lead to the erosion of promptness and affect adversely the quality of decision-making. Unfortunately, in the Government there are as many as 35 persons or departments in several cases who have to decide whether to agree to a particular proposal or not. All of them have the veto power to say 'No' without being responsible for the consequences of their actions. The leader's job is to ensure that the work he has undertaken is completed on schedule.

> Faith and patience are the foundations of all endeavours, relationships and ultimate success.

You should make sure that there is a fixed time limit for every task. No work should be assigned on a loose-ended basis. This way you will get more done in less time. It will definitely be more than those who dodge taking decisions. Listening is more important than recounting your own experiences. You should form a habit of listening without interrupting, without prejudices and without forming any opinions. A satisfied and a motivated staff in an organization can achieve results far superior than those who are not happy or are disgruntled. Use of the latest technology or the most sophisticated equipment is only an aid. It cannot replace individuals.

A successful person will always know by intuition that he can bargain or negotiate only up to the limit set by the other person. He will dress in accordance with his position and the workplace. Many a time he will be known by the clothes and shoes he wears. He does not dress only for comfort but also in accordance with the norms of decency. Dressing has to be appropriate, befitting, comfortable, decent and elegant. In other words, a successful person does not forget the ABC of the dress code. An overdressed person can be as much of an embarrassment as a bizarre or a sloppily dressed individual. Good manners in dressing are as important as conduct and behaviour. A success-oriented person knows that a lot of stress in our life occurs due to non-fulfilment of strongly felt desires and wishes.

A suppressed desire including worry leads to a lot of problems. Worry has a habit of magnifying trifles into big problems. A successful person will deal with all his problems as they arise and will give his best.

Faith and patience are the foundations of all endeavours, relationships and ultimate success. Everything blossoms and comes to fruition in its own time. However, patience should not be allowed to be used as an excuse for not making efforts to succeed in one's goal. No excuse is good enough for finding new ways of doing things better. Patience is a willingness to suppress annoyance and impatience. We get annoyed when things do not move the way we want them to move. Facing delay can also lead to impatience. Patience itself is quiet perseverance and diligence. It is one quality whose success feeds on itself. We must be on the look out for alternatives rather than sit around doing nothing. The impatience to reach goals without sufficient hard work and planning is an obsession with most people. It extends to all aspects of modern life. Most people take short cuts to success. They expect miracles. They also want quick cures and instant solutions to all problems. We get edgy and impatient when we are thwarted. There are no quick fixes in human relationships. All of us want to have our say. Sometimes people keep on interrupting others to say what they want to. I had a service colleague who would always hold the floor almost to the point of ransom. He made himself obnoxious by not letting complete even one sentence during the conversation. Nobody liked him for this trait though otherwise he was a first rate individual. He did not have the social courtesy and patience to allow others to have their say. He was only an attentive speaker and not a listener.

> ★ Acceptance of the world and people around us is an important concomitant of patience.

It is always better even from a practical point of view to listen to others. Once I was invited as a guest speaker to an important function. I asked the hosts to send me some material on the subject I was expected to speak on. My host also did not have the material. He suggested that I preside over the function and be the last speaker. He added that I should listen to others, take notes and then speak from whichever side I wanted to. I agreed to do so. It gave me enough time to collect my thoughts and time to present a cogent point of view. Thus, I was much better prepared to speak and appear as an expert than if I had been impatient. This was possible only by patiently listening to others. Patience means bearing provocation, annoyance, misfortune and pain without complaining, loss of temper and irritation. It is the willingness to suppress annoyance when confronted with unpleasant situations.

Patience is also a quiet perseverance and a sort of diligence. It is the pre-requisite to success and multiplies itself. It is a quality of the head and heart. It needs a deliberate and constant practice to thrive. Fortitude is a step further. It is patience with strength of character when faced with pain, afflictions and hardship. Stoicism is calm fortitude. It may at times look like indifference. Impatience often manifests itself in the form of being jumpy, nervous, edgy, pacing up and down a room, speaking fast, losing temper etc. Impatience makes a person so stressed that he cannot think straight. His response becomes either sluggish or like a fired cannon ball. We should learn to create patience practice sessions so that we do not sweat at the small stuff. This is the only way to keep things in their proper perspective. This quality even in an emergency will emit so much confidence that no life-and-death situation can compare with it. This approach will enable us to use our mental and physical resources in a manner in which we will come up with viable, practical and sensible solutions to our problems. A patient person is always peaceful and radiates love and affection. He is not a cribber, full of regrets about what ought to have been. He makes the best of a bad situation and never gets frustrated because he has added the dimension of ease and acceptance to his life. Acceptance of the world and people around us is an important concomitant of patience. Also, patience generates happiness through the development of inner peace even in the face of challenges and difficulties. It can change people and situations which no impatient, hustling, coercion, threatening, kicking and bashing around can ever achieve.

Patience has many rewards. It must be understood that each one of us has a role to play in the world. We can only play our own role. We can only do our job well. The important thing is that the entire system should work well and yield results. There are certain situations in life which depend on us and there are others which depend on others. If, for instance, your plane or train is delayed or you are caught in a traffic jam there is nothing you can do except wait for the situation to untangle itself. Being impatient does not lead to any solution. The acid test should be to ask yourself whether you can do anything to change the situation and do damage control. If the answer is 'Yes' find a way to tackle events and improve upon a situation. If it is 'Cannot be done', it is best to wait patiently and do something constructive with the time which has become available. Avoid having an impatience or panic attack. Both in impatience and nervousness, logic and reason are the first casualties. It is important to be effective and do things effectively but it may not always be the quickest way of doing things. Effectiveness has many facets. One of them is insufficient thought and planning. So, in an emergency it is more important to be calm and collected rather than hurriedly trying to straighten things out. It is true that we are never fully contented in life. When one desire is achieved another one crops up. We always want to achieve just a little more. In fact, it is this which has led to all progress and development in life. No progress in life will be possible if we feel satisfied. Ambition and hard work are the ladders of success. It is hard work which has a unique pleasure of its own. But once one has done one's best one must learn to be content. Most people view any impending change as a threat without realizing that ultimately it may turn out to be the best thing to have happened to them. Faith in yourself is essential to success and happiness. Success and failure are both in the mind. It is your own thinking which leads you to success or failure. Structure environments and conditions around you to succeed rather than to fail. There is no such thing as the best one size that is relevant to all solutions to any difficulty. It is your attitude that determines your future. Have a strategy ready for dealing with any problem you might face or a conflict you might have to manage.

Patience helps in eliminating small irritations. Usually most of us focus on trifles, small problems and insignificant concerns. We give them importance out of proportion to what they really deserve. In the interests of long-term goals and objectives it is better to remain patient both in the present and the future. It is prudent, for instance, to suffer the temper tantrums and unreasonable behaviour of your spouse or a boss and then point out gently the rationale of your action or behaviour in a particular situation. Nothing is gained in reacting, losing your cool or walking out in a huff. Keeping one's cool, sticking around till the storm blows over and then going one's own way is the best alternative. This holds true for both professional and personal conduct. You should believe in the triumph of patience over others' impertinence. It is easy to get along famously with like-minded people. The real triumph is to deal with unreasonable people and suffer the company of fools. The challenge lies in tackling them with grace and dignity. Patience like mulberry ultimately becomes silk.

Neither A Borrower, Nor A Lender Be

One problem we all face is that of people who wish to borrow things from us, including our video, audio cassettes and CDs. One should stock one's own video and audio things and not use others'. As the problem of space stares at most of us, it is wise to ask whether a book, CD, or a video might be available as and when required. My own experience has shown that I myself have not used some of my own music CDs or audio and video cassettes for years. Yet they occupy prime space in my study. I doubt whether I will ever have the time, or inclination to listen to them. The ones I wanted to watch have outlived their utility. Yet, we have such a preservationist culture in India that we will not get rid of most things. It is wise to go through one's entire books and media library once a year. It is best to either sell, donate and discard anything that has ceased to be interesting and informative.

Most of us purchase some newspapers or magazines. A magazine is a kind of contemporary history. It is a compressed newspaper of incidents or happenings which have occurred in the last fortnight or month. We are tempted to retain some old publications. When you are tempted to retain it, ask yourself whether you want to keep it as a memento or for use later on. It is best to scan the items, if you have a computer and a scanner, instead of cluttering your place with papers. Also, ask yourself that in case you needed the magazine again, could you get it from the lending library. What happens in actual practice is that

> ★ Goals should be creative, service-oriented and conform to the expectations of society.

some article fascinates us whatever be the subject. We want to preserve the whole magazine. The best way would be to cut out the article and sell the remaining magazine. In our country, fortunately, there is still a market for junk. In Europe and the USA you have to pay for getting the junk removed. No papers except National Awards or certificates are fit to be preserved. Most magazines and newspapers are of interest only for a limited period. Store your magazines and newspapers in vertical, see-through magazine boxes made of wire. This way you can see and replace the periodicals which have outlived their utility. If you must preserve the clipped articles, preserve the same in transparent folders or notebooks classified according to subjects, whether it is crime, politics, gardening or stamp collection with dividers for sub-categories. These are some of the ways to keep yourself well-organized.

Get The Best What Life Has To Offer

One of the great blessings of life is friendship. It is a two-way traffic. But to have a good friend and be a good friend is interconnected. It is a link in the chain of life. Acquiring and being a good friend is not difficult. Friends are made by many actions and lost only by one. Having money and friendship is easy. Having friends and no money is an accomplishment. Maintaining friendship needs wisdom and cleverness. Friendship needs to be based on understanding, an ability to appreciate each other's point of view, tolerance and an element of sacrifice. It also requires a genuine interest in your friend's welfare and measures exactly to the same degree as you would like him to be interested in you.

An aimless life generates despair. A person with some objective and aim which he desperately wants to achieve will never be bored in life. It is being interested in life and targeting for an aim which keeps us active and going. After achieving one goal we should move on to another one to make life rewarding. Goals should be creative, service-oriented and conform to the expectations of society. Being honest in the performance of one's duties is serving society. The company that one keeps or the friends that one has shows a person's standing and character. Without friends most people feel lonely, miserable and unhappy. Minor troubles get magnified into and small difficulties get blown up as giant problems when we do not have friends. "No man is useless while he has a friend and a well-wisher." Friendship provides comfort in distress. It is also a source of great joy in happy times.

Be a friend in whom others can confide their sorrows and misfortunes. Be a comrade and give help, advice and guidance. Share your joys, fortunes and good deeds and multiply happiness. Listening and encouraging others to talk reduces the magnitude of their sorrow. Ask questions to lighten the burdens of others. Speak and listen to others with interest and enthusiasm. The blame game never pays. If you have to play it then it is better done in private. Praise in public acts as a tonic. Appreciate your friend's achievements as you would like him to appreciate yours. Share your joyous moments as well as the secrets of success with your friend. Discuss the struggles he has undergone. It will go a long way in cementing friendship and understanding. A smile can almost win everybody. It is the best antidote to depression. A frown will almost never help you make friends and may perhaps make you lose the existing ones.

Respect others' opinions and ideas though you may not agree with them. Honour the confidence reposed in you and be loyal to yourself and your friends. Always be there for your friends. Mutual help and assistance is invaluable. Never keep friends waiting. It is a sure way to antagonize them. Nobody likes to be treated as an inferior. Apologize if you offend anybody. It will win both appreciation and respect. Always be fair in your dealings. It will create a sense of confidence. Life is a great teacher. Everyday it teaches us new lessons from the book of experience. Its feedback inspires us to work continuously for achieving greater and greater heights. During our lifetime we pass through various tunnels, turns and bad patches. Life occasionally exposes us to sorrows and unhappiness. It is entirely up to us not to feel discouraged and disheartened. At every such turn a new path to happiness and joy starts. The only requirement is that we should be vigilant so that we do not miss the right turn. Our friends can be of great help in such contingencies. Life never stands still. Hope is the soul of our existence. The world is based on hope and faith. Life, hope and faith go together. It is the expectation and hope for a better existence which has led to the evolution and development of man to his present stature. The products of man's intelligence, competence and ability have made our lives full of comfort and conveniences. If there was no compassion none of the several inventions, discoveries and advances in medical sciences would have been possible which have reduced man's pain and suffering.

An ideal mode to live a friction free life is possible only with a lot of support and friendship. There will always be storms which will threaten to drown the

> ★ Life without love is meaningless.

boat of life. But friendship which is the sweetest song in life is waiting to be played. It is for us to play it. Friendship is the greatest gift of God to human beings. A true friend will always stand by us in the moments we need him most. Life without a friend is just like a temple without God. Friendship acts as a lubrication to smoothen the rough edges of life. Friendship and love make life worth living. Life without love is meaningless. It is the love for achieving high status and wealth which makes people work hard. It is just like the love for the country that inspires a person to lay down his life for it. It is the desire for excellence which has led to the new inventions and discoveries in almost every sphere of human acuity.

If you want the best out of your life, give your best to every role or job you that have to do. Aim to be a role model for others whether it is the role of a son, a brother, a husband, a father, a colleague, a boss or that of a citizen. Never be rude and ill-mannered. You should also not be unjust. You have every right to enjoy your rights but you should not create any problem for others. Observe 'lakshman rekhas' or the sacred boundaries in all walks of your life. Keep an eye on the working of the government as an active citizen. Shakespeare said, "What wound did ever heal but by patience." Patience is the art of hoping and persevering even against heavy odds. It is the art of keeping on trying again and again despite repeated failures even in the worst of circumstances. Lord Krishna said that if a person follows the right path and his goal patiently without deviating from his course he will ultimately achieve his objective. Good times and bad times keep on criss-crossing life all the time. Never be disheartened in adverse circumstances. Never leave your task or work on the grounds that life or circumstances are impossible and unfair. The correct spelling of the word 'impossible' is "I'm possible."

Always cling to your visions and lofty ideals with patience, perseverance and an iron will. It is not necessary that before starting the journey you should be able to see the end of the road. What is important in the journey of life is to see that your next step is in the right direction. Difficulties are meant to rouse us to action and not to discourage us. The lowest ebb is the beginning of the turn of the tide for all of us. We can learn a lesson from the postage stamp. Its utility lies in its ability to stick to an envelope or a parcel until it gets to its destination. We can also do anything if we stick to it patiently, resolutely and long enough. We should never be afraid of growing slowly. We should guard against standing still. Success in life is only a matter of patience. Whenever you feel depressingly slow in your progress in the journey of life remember that everything in life takes its time. It is very important for people to know what you stand for. It is more important also for your colleagues, superiors, subordinates, friends and relations to know what you would always do and the things that you would never do.

Joy Zone

Relationships in every walk of life are the most important facets of human existence. Good relationships should not be discarded either on the spur of the moment or on an emotional upsurge. It is important to maintain a balance between various requirements in life. It is the responsibility of the top man to encourage innovations. He must also provide support and resources to encourage commitment to the objectives of the organization. The top man should also encourage a system which determines, recognizes and rewards innovations. We perceive and react according to the way in which we think. Do not be afraid of getting lost in your quest. All journeys will reveal something new. It may, ultimately, turn out to be the best thing to have happened. For success one has to learn to be audacious and willing to experiment. Sometimes audacity can lead to new avenues and opportunities. Worry has no place in rationality. Winners are positive by nature. They are always willing to try out new ideas and new challenges. They are always on the look out for discovering new ways of performing better. They always learn something new from every experience. They know that the best way to succeed is to keep learning and improving their skills.

You can also learn something new everyday if you pay attention to what is happening around you. When you make a mistake and realize it, then rectify it quickly. It is easier to do so immediately. Delay hardens attitudes. Be always in harmony with yourself, your environment and surroundings. It is problem-solving which keeps us happy and occupied. There should be sufficient work and sufficient problems. This is the only way to ensure happiness. Too little work and too few problems pose no challenge and bore us. If there is too much to do we can sometimes be overwhelmed and feel that solving any problem or challenge is beyond our capacity or competence. It is necessary to devise a system of dealing with the problems. It is bound

> Original thinking and continuous learning should always be given top priority and rewarded.

to vary from individual to individual. People and places are always the richest resources. It is best to have a system which encourages an environment where each individual will feel motivated to give his best to achieve the goals of the organization. Original thinking and continuous learning should always be given top priority and rewarded. A culture of pride and the core values of the organization for which one is working should be developed. Core values and pride in the job are the basis of all achievements. The management of any group should always strive to create a conducive atmosphere for all employees. In the case of women employees their complaints of harassment and discrimination should be taken seriously. Special attention should be paid to the problem of sexual harassment in case there is any such complaint from them. A culture should be developed where everybody's views are heard and the leadership trusted.

There are warriors in every field. There is a basic difference between a warrior and an ordinary person. A warrior will meet any problem as a challenge. An ordinary person will consider any problem or a happening either as a blessing or a curse. There is certainly a better way to deal with anything. All experiences should be converted into something constructive. Success comes not from the experience but what one does with the experience. Good judgement and experience are intertwined. Making mistakes may result in an experience which can be a guiding star in the future. It is putting the experience to good use which results in good judgement. Roles and expectations in our life keep on changing and are redefined from time to time. The traditional role in which any generation is brought up is not always valid or practical for all times to come. Use every opportunity to compliment, commend and congratulate yourself, your colleagues, partners and fellow workers even on small accomplishments. Lavish praise at all conceivable opportunities. Compliments always deepen love. Nourish self-esteem and make every relationship a lovely one. Small gestures convey large and meaningful signals. "Raised voices lower self esteem. Hot tempers cool friendships. Loose tongues stretch truth. Sharp words dull respect."

You must learn to spend a large chunk of your time with your family. This will keep the family together and smoothen out any rough edges. Share your happy moments. Do your share of the work. This will avoid any hard feelings as resentment builds up quickly when only one person has to work harder than others in the same organization. Be patient. The key to everything is patience. You get the chicken by hatching the egg and not by smashing it. Give the benefit of doubt in the interest of peace and calm. When you are in the wrong do not hesitate to apologize. When you are right, do not be self-righteous and be silent.

The Things We Should Be Doing

It is always best to have an audit of your own performance periodically so that the shortcomings of the past are not repeated. It is alright to improve the world but charity should begin at home with each one of us. The world can become a better place only if we do better in our own limited sphere of life. One thing which all of us can do is to be punctual to the dot. It will make life easier for ourselves as well as for those we come in contact with. Whether it is a government or a social function like a dinner or a marriage party a delay from one hour to four hours is not only taken for granted but also accepted without a murmur. One way to deal with this kind of a problem is to be punctual yourself. Once when posted in Bangalore I hosted a dinner and invited a few friends. Since I am a teetotaller and sleep early I do not go in for late dinners and parties. Even socialization has a tolerance and boredom threshold. If it is in excess, instead of offering pleasure such occasions become a pain in the neck. After some time all the topics of conversation, the weather, the last party which figured on page 3 of the newspapers are exhausted. I have a standard schedule for all parties which I host. They normally start at 8 pm in summer and 7.30 pm in winter. On arrival of the guests cold drinks or juice and snacks are served. I do not serve any liquor and this is well known to all the guests. Pre-dinner soup is served between 9 and 9.15 pm for those who wish to help themselves and dinner is announced at 9.30 pm.

The whole party is over by 10.30 pm and people leave. I had a problem with a friend who if at all he came would turn up almost at the fag-end of most of my dinners. He knew that I did not like gross unpunctuality. One day he turned up at 10.30 pm for dinner when all the guests were leaving. I asked my servant in a loud voice whether there was any food left or would we have to get the food from the market. He said, "Sir, only some food is left for the servants and the drivers. It is better that you take your friend out for dinner to a restaurant." My visitor sheepishly apologized for coming late and said that he had had gone for another dinner and hence he was late. I offered to take him out for dinner though it was 11 pm which he mercifully declined on the ground that he had had his dinner.

Actually he had not gone anywhere and had not eaten his dinner. But it cured him of unpunctuality as far as any future invitation from me was concerned. Lack of punctuality is a lack of consideration for others. It is also important that what each one of us does to others should be what we would like others to do to us.

It is a common practice that in most market and residential areas people throw garbage in the centre of the road or in front of other people's houses or shops. It is the easiest thing to pass on the buck to the Municipal Corporation and say it is their duty to do it. It may be their duty to collect garbage but it is our duty to dump the garbage in the garbage collection bin.

Punctuality and consideration for others are the hallmark of a person who values himself and others. Keep yourself open to new ideas and do not be defensive about your ways of doing things. If you continue to live in the past you will become a fossil. Surely punctuality and consideration for others will never become outdated.

How To Do More By Listening To Your Body

God has made each human being different. There are some people who bounce off their bed at 5 am and straightaway go for exercises like jogging, golfing, gymnasium or some other workout. Such persons after a hectic morning, shower, take breakfast and rush to work full of enthusiasm. Others in the same family wake up at the last possible

The fact is that there is no right or wrong way to live or work.

minute, reluctantly drag themselves to finish the morning routine and literally drag themselves to work. My two daughters Randeep and Gagandeep are exactly in the same category but both are professionally competent and happy. The fact is that there is no right or wrong way to live or work. It is a simple question of how we are and how our body clock functions or regulates itself. To get the best out of oneself one should identify one's peak performance times and use that time to do one's best or prime work. This is the only way to use your time and body clock to your advantage. Hopefully, it will be a few times during the day otherwise you will have a problem.

For an early bird or when you feel most active it makes sense to do the hardest tasks the first thing in the morning. That will mean that you work on a specific task or a project or do anything which requires concentration and attention. It is a sheer waste of time to do routine work in your peak hour of energy. Take up the routine work when you begin to feel tired or lose concentration. This could be in the form of organizing meetings, attending to visitors or keeping appointments at a time when you have nearly run out of steam. Meetings planned for late afternoon especially near closing time tend to be shorter as everyone wants to get home. You can also make your phone calls and attend to other routine work like e-mail during this time.

Some people like me are late starters. I am the reverse of the early bird. Going for a run or walk at 5.00 am is just not on my agenda. My best time for work is after lunch and rest. I have to drag myself if I have to have an early start which includes catching an early morning plane or a train. In fact, I do not accept any engagements in the forenoon. I am best at handling serious work in the afternoon. The result is that to make best use of my time I prefer to meet people in the morning or read newspapers. I recognize that everyone is different and has different peak hours. The trick of successful men or women lies in recognizing their high energy times and planning their work accordingly for maximum achievement. A few tips like changing your position from sitting up to standing up, drinking plenty of water (a minimum of 8 glasses a day is invigorating) walking up to see a colleague, switching to an easier task, doing deep breathing and going outside your working place for a breath of fresh air, cleaning up your workplace or even taking a short nap will give your mind and body a break. Such a break can give up to three hours of fresh energy. Your diet and exercise regimem play a tremendous role in keeping your energy level high. They enable you to have a high quality of life with unbounded energy levels, enthusiasm and self-esteem, irrespective of the fact that you are an early bird or a late starter. Developing yourself is a constant task that involves constant endeavour. One needs to grow and develop oneself for the future. Have a plan for your personal and professional development for the next 180 days. It will also mean doing fresh courses, reading new books and learning from others. It will mean planning events, using tips, practical strategies, systems and suggestions to meet new challenges.

Rules Of Good Living

These days so-called frankness and candour borders on rudeness, incivility and arrogance. Abrasive hostility and downright contempt for others is what characterizes not only the younger generation but also a vast majority of snobs. We have forgotten that every action in the company of others should be done with some sign of respect and consideration for those present. There is nothing quaint or ancient about basic good manners. Good manners have not altered during the ages and will not in the times to come. Despite the widespread craze for material goods it is essential for each one of us to keep alive that small fire called 'conscience'. George Washington had the following rules written down. He referred to them all his life. Most of them are still valid. One: Do not clean your teeth with the tablecloth and do not rinse your mouth in the presence of others. Two: Do not spit into the fire. Three: Do not remove your clothes in the presence of others. Four: Do not laugh too much or too loudly in a public place. Five: Do not scratch your private parts in public.

It is a good saying that as we sow so shall we reap. Happiness, joy, goodness, love and kindness generously scattered in life will multiply in abundance. It is our actions which bring about justice or injustice or nemesis to us. When we do good to others, it makes us feel good. It benefits us mentally, physically and spiritually. We should learn to be on best terms with ourselves. We should constantly monitor our own thinking process to ensure that only positive and pleasant thoughts stay in our subconscious mind. Our thoughts and the way we focus on them determine our destiny. All success in our life depends on how we tackle our thinking process. Try to live life effortlessly and avoid collisions of values and principles. Controlling our thinking process helps us control our own destiny. "Nothing is good or bad but thinking makes it so."

> The best approach is to sort out the issues in the open.

The way of the world is to recognize and salute the rising sun. Nobody even talks about the sun which has set as to how hot or glorious it was yesterday. It is true in the affairs of men. Most magazines and journals ask successful people the secret of reaching the heights they have reached. Moneybags are lionized everywhere. The rich man's idiosyncrasies and frailties are magnified as something personal or something worth to be copied and not something to be avoided. Their dress style, method of living and working have become role models for others who copy them in the hope that they will reach the same position as their idols by exactly copying them in an unthinking manner. This exercise is carried even to the point of imitating their tantrums and eating and living habits.

Nobody is perfect and the methods of success adopted by one person will not suit someone else. This is because everybody works in a different milieu and a different environment. While copying others the fact should not be forgotten that each one of us works with a different set of circumstances, different people and an entirely different commitment or approach. Promoting commitment, encouraging perseverance and motivating people in an organization is of utmost importance. Occasionally, one may have to change the way of working because of unpredictable changes The trick lies in being responsive to change. An important part of teamwork is listening to others' point of view and not steamrolling them. Success comes through networking as a team and giving one's best for achieving set goals. The best approach is to sort out the issues in the open. When you try to achieve a lot you should also be ready to change in accordance with your vision to maintain the strategic focus. It is important to diffuse destructive situations to move forward positively.

No relationship between two individuals is perfect. All relationships have their bouts of discord, doubts, distortions, misinterpretations, misunderstandings and bumps. Never quit in desperation, exasperation and frustration though it may appear to be the easiest approach. Only perseverance, grit and resolute determination can help you gain everything worthwhile in life. All rewards in life go only to those who persevere till they succeed. You can never succeed with a half-hearted approach. Iron out whatever comes in the way of achievement. Human beings are extraordinarily different. We all need to be reasonably good psychologists so that we can predict and anticipate as to how other persons will react to a given situation.

Only people with sufficient motivation can become agents of change. However, organizations need to become more conscious of the needs of the people for whom they are created. From time to time workers' performance has to be reviewed to meet the goals of the organization and a continued restructuring is needed. This is done by either cutting down on staff for effective management, or empowering them, depending upon the functions to be performed.

Changes are usually unpredictable but some can be anticipated except in some organizations which do not punish failure. There can be a mental block in dealing with failures. The best course in life is to chart your own destiny by your own competence and hard work. Never fall into the trap that the world owes you a living. In some cases it is the degree of competition which challenges you to effort. Innovation is the essence of life.

> ★ With enthusiasm you can conquer the entire world and also the sky if you wish.

Leadership consists in understanding people and getting them to work in the same direction for achieving common objectives. It is also the making of strategic choices, decisions and having a vision which will bind people together in an organization towards achieving objectives. The responsibility of an orderly and desired change lies only with the leaders. The leader depending upon a set of given circumstances or approach can exercise the power of punishment, coercion or rewards. The underlying idea of all such actions is to attain set goals. A combination of youthful energy and experience of the mature is still the best combination. Bossing warns that an authoritarian attitude does not always work. The best worker can still get a better placement if he is forced to quit or is pushed around. Competence always gets a placement though change is always resisted. A lot of labour in the form of adequate planning, brainstorming, new ideas, understanding the current situation, preparation and evaluation of the impact of the change should go into any exercise which consciously decides about a change. Effective communication is essential so that the persons affected become partners in change rather than hostile bystanders. Upgrading skills and knowledge should be built into all organizations which target better and higher goals. This will give you confidence and this in turn will have a multiplier effect in generating enthusiasm. With enthusiasm you can conquer the entire world and also the sky if you wish . The willingness to take risks also includes some built-in apprehensions of fear and failure. Without risk you cannot even drive on the road. The present should be made both attractive and exciting to spur people on to new challenges for a still better future. Any initiative entails cost in terms of money, time as well as challenges from colleagues and competitors.

Initiative should be fast enough to catch emerging opportunities. For success there has to be a blend of ideas, innovative culture and a style that will achieve results. In the process the old rules, conventions and practices should be jettisoned for attainment of new goals and objectives.

For success it is better to change by choice and not by coercion, accident or chance. With a clockwise regularity, orders and directives are issued both in the government and the private sector to achieve higher targets or to change the way matters are handled. Change is always resisted. The reasons for resisting change can be lack of motivation, lack of training or poor comprehension. Another important reason why government employees resist change is that the government takes away the discretion of the employees and prevents the corrupt from indulging in corrupt practices. On the other hand, there can be an honest, different opinion about a contemplated change. There is a human tendency to evaluate as to what effect any change will have on one's efficiency, approach or commitment to work. Individual reaction is bound to be different in different cases. The best course would be to explain the rationale for change. A clear verbal clarification will go a long way for getting things moving in the desired direction.

For achieving success in any organization it is essential to spot out the weak and unsuccessful and inefficient links and then concentrate on improving those areas.

> ★ Learn to take criticism effectively.

It is always better to have the communication lines open so that there is no room for misunderstanding and you can give your best. Goals must be clear. It should be emphasized that the desired change is carefully planned and explained to those charged with implementing it. Competition in a way is responsible for innovation, creativity and flexibility of approach in striving for excellence in more than one way. The ability to respond to change is a key factor for meeting the challenge of competitors. It is challenge which captures the imagination, enthusiasm and intellectual capital. Performance should be appraised regularly to meet the target. The best performance appraisal procedures available should be applied. It is true that an individual can never be in full control of conditions which impinge upon his performance which is dependent on the environment as well as the goals set and the methods and procedure laid down to achieve them by the organization . In most organizations attitudes and behaviour are structured. Total achievement depends on the performance of various segments.

When you ask leading questions do it with a view to direct the conversation to what you want to know rather than what you want to hear. It is better to resist the temptation of giving advice. Unless people ask for advice, do not impose your opinions on them as to how to solve their problems. When conversing do not agree or disagree with what others say no matter what your own opinions are. It is best not to be defensive and react as such even if some views and opinions bother you. Clichés are meaningless. Cut them out of your life. Learn to take criticism effectively. Do not react emotionally to any criticism.

First impressions are lasting. Your effort should be to make a lasting impression. You should be a self-starter and a problem solver. You should stay organized everyday. When you speak, have something meaningful to say. Always develop a taste for winning and succeeding. You should always anticipate things. Anticipation of what is going to happen is as important as what happens. Shakespeare has said, "There is nothing good or bad but thinking makes it so." Though we live in the body it is the mind which controls it. There is no way you can do anything unless you conceive of it in your mind. All fear, worries and successes have their origin in the mind. The only ladder to success and overcoming carelessness, disorganization and negative thinking is through development of confidence in your own ability. Never accept defeat. Do not resign yourself to failure. You can take a number of steps to live life to the full in the time given to you. Be aware of your shortcomings. Do not accept them. Do something for better conditioning and achievement. You can devise your own ways of improving your thinking and approach in life. I, for instance, write down any good or inspiring thoughts and memorize them. I have made audio-tapes of my own positive writings and those of others. I listen to them on my Walkman tape recorder when travelling, bathing or during my morning walk. This peps me up.

Another friend of mine starts his day by visiting a holy place. Yet another listens to religious discourses and hymns. The possibilities are limitless. It all depends on how you view your life. Life is constantly in a state of flux. There can be no permanent guarantee in our life neither of our life span nor of relationships. Your aim should be to get the maximum out of this limited span. You yourself can be the best pillar on which to support your life. Only you can overcome the attitude of fear, hopelessness and despair. You have to work out your own strategy. Never be cynical. In life and business quite often we have to traverse unknown horizons. In the struggle for life, new and revolutionary approaches should be tried. The future for every generation is both exciting and fascinating. There is no way anyone can stall the future. Plan for getting to the future first by learning and innovating in this highly competitive world. Every action of ours affects something, our family or an organization. It may not manifest directly and immediately but it does so in one form or the other. The future is flexible, fast moving and offers new opportunities. Change is going to happen as it is the law of life. Better welcome it and be prepared to move with the times by reorienting your priorities and enhancing efficiency all around.

Keep Smiling

At times we must learn to philosophically accept God's will. We should not allow unfulfilled desires to disfigure our mind. As an achiever you have to take rejections in your stride, for example, being thrown out of a job. You may see your favourite ideas flounder. You have to learn to carve out opportunities from adverse circumstances. Failures should not prevent and discourage you from doing what you want to achieve. They should spur you to greater achievements. Persistence is the backbone and bedrock of success. At times even the most persistent person can feel overwhelmed. He may feel like throwing in the towel and giving in. A successful leap comes through one step at a time. A successful person stays zeroed to his target. For achieving success Irwin Hansen said, "All you need is a big pot of glue. You smear some on your chair and some on the seat of your pants, you sit down and you stick with every project until you have done the best you can."

> What matters is our outlook on life.

A successful man should not and generally does not carry any excess baggage in the form of pre-conceived notions in his relationships with others. A success-oriented person knows that there will always be differences in education, social, cultural upbringing and personal approach among people. He knows and realizes that there are bound to be differences in the way people make adjustments, compromises or reduce friction and resolve differences. A successful person is a happy man. He is aware that every day he has only two choices. He can either choose to be happy or unhappy. He invariably chooses to be happy. He does not manufacture his own happiness. He as a matter of habit and principle manufactures happiness. He develops a happiness habit. He does this by practising happiness. He allows only positive and happy thoughts to pass through and stay in his mind. He does not allow any depressing and unhappy thoughts to enter his mind. If by chance they find an entry they are immediately ejected and replaced by happy thoughts.

Life is the same for the good as well as the bad. What matters is our outlook on life. A happy individual has the ability to turn his present existence into a heaven. An unhappy man can turn his life with the same set of circumstances into hell. Life is not a mathematical or scientific formula. Lifestyles differ from individual to individual as each individual lives in his own way. We live it and make a success of it as we go along. Each one of us has the power to be happy. There is nothing to be ashamed of in copying the lifestyle of happy persons and learning from them how to remain happy.

According to Peale, "The way to happiness is: To keep your heart free from hate, your mind from worry. Live simply, expect little and give much. Fill your life with love. Scatter sunshine. Forget yourself and think of others. Do as you would be done by." The art of personal interaction and relationships with others is vital to success. Sometimes out of sheer fear of being misunderstood and possible humiliation we abstain from showing our best side. A sense of humour and ability to laugh at ourselves is a good balm. Do not hold yourself back. Never laugh at another person's expense. Gracefully accept and listen to the other person's point of view. Never be jealous of others. For getting the best results your daily programme should be planned, scheduled and executed to the best of your ability and intelligence. This will give you control over your life.

While working for the government in several capacities as Director in the Ministry of Commerce, or DIG or IG of Police or as Director, CBI, I noticed that I worked on the proposal files, programmes and projects which were put up to me during my first ten years of service. I realized frequently at the end of the day that I had only meandered along. I started the practice of daily planning first thing in the morning. I would write down everything to be done. When I joined the CBI my list would include even ordinary work like polishing shoes to dealing with the fodder or urea scam or Bofors case. I noticed that it increased my output by at least 400%. I had the satisfaction of having stayed focused on the things I wanted to do. I could get more done in far less time than I imagined. I was considered more competent, as management is essentially a system of putting competencies of different people in various walks of life together. I could devise a method in my working and bring

> Each adversity has its positive aspect.

order out of the chaos of running from one place to another for meetings, phone calls and files.

Emerson rightly said, "Every excess causes a defeat in excess. Everything sweet is sour; every evil is good. Every faculty which is a receiver of pleasure has an equal penalty put on its abuse. It is to answer for its moderation with its life. For every grain of wit there is a grain of folly. For everything you have missed you have gained something else; and for everything you gain you lose something. If riches increase they are increased for those that use them. If the gatherer gathers too much, nature takes out of the man what she puts into his chest; it swells the estate that kills the owner. Nature hates monopolies and exceptions. The waves of the sea do not more speedily seek a level from their loftiest tossing than the varieties of condition which tend to equalize themselves. There are always some levelling circumstances that put down the overbearing, the strong, the rich, the fortunate, the substantial on the same ground with everyone else." Each adversity has its positive aspect. The changes which break up at short intervals the prosperity of men are advertisements of nature whose law is growth. Moreover, it is the order of nature to grow and every soul is by intrinsic necessity quitting its whole system of things, its friends and home, laws and faith like the shellfish which crawls out of its beautiful but stony case because it no longer admits of its growth and slowly forms a new house. And yet the compensations of calamity are made apparent to the understanding also after long intervals of time.

A fever, a mutilation, a cruel disappointment, loss of wealth or of friends seems at the moment unpaid loss and unpayable. But the years reveal the deep remedial force that underlies all facts. The death of a dear friend, wife, brother or lover which seemed nothing but sorrow at the time, somewhat later commonly creates a revolution in our way of life. It terminates an epoch of infancy or of youth which was waiting to be closed, breaks up an occupation or a household or a style of living and allows the formation of new ways, more friendly to the growth of character. It permits or constraints the formation of new acquaintances and the reception of new influences that prove of great importance in time to come.

In other words there is no unmitigated disaster in life. So cheer up and take life as it comes and make the best of it. It happens all the time that if the things do not go by our way we judge it as our total failure. Our judgement is coloured by our own expectations. A disaster is only a mixed blessing. During the partition of the country in 1947 the Punjab state lost its capital Lahore, to Pakistan. But within five years the state went in for building its own capital, Chandigarh. It is one of the best planned cities and the pride of India. The 1962 war with China was a disaster for the country but it enabled the nation to prepare itself for any eventuality. The result was that it emerged as a winner in the 1965, 1971 and 1999 wars with Pakistan. Every event, every activity in life can teach us to face the future more confidently and purposefully. It can happen to each one of us provided we learn from our failures. The trick is not to repeat mistakes and do our best always.

> ★ The trick is not to repeat mistakes and do your best always.

Join the
WORLD
WISDOM BOOK CLUB

Get the best of world literature in the comfort of your home at fabulous discounts!

Benefits of the Book Club

Wherever in the world you are, you can receive the best of books at your doorstep.

- Receive FABULOUS DISCOUNTS by mail or at the FULL CIRCLE Store in Delhi.
- Receive Exclusive Invitations to attend events being organized by FULL CIRCLE.
- Receive a FREE copy of the club newsletter — The World Wisdom Review — every month.
- Get UPTO 25% OFF.

Join Now!

Its simple. Just fill in the coupon below and mail it to us at the given address:

Yes, I would like to be a member of the World Wisdom Book Club

Name ☐ Mr ☐ Mrs ☐ Ms _____

Mailing Address _____

_____

City _____ Pin _____

Phone _____ Fax _____

E-mail _____

Profession _____ D.O.B. _____

Areas of Interest _____

_____

Mail this form to:
The World Wisdom Book Club
J-40, Jorbagh Lane, New Delhi - 110003 • Tel. : 24620063, 55654197-98 • Fax: 24645795
E-mail: fullcircle@vsnl.com / gbp@del2.vsnl.net.in